MW00782687

モノクル日本全集

The Monocle Book of
JAPAN

First published in the United Kingdom in 2020
by MONOCLE and Thames & Hudson Ltd,
181A High Holborn, London, WC1V 7QX
thamesandhudson.com

First published in the United States of America in 2020
by MONOCLE and Thames & Hudson Inc,
500 Fifth Avenue, New York, New York, 10110
thamesandhudsonusa.com

MONOCLE is a trading name of Winkontent Limited

© 2020 Winkontent Limited of Midori House,
1 Dorset Street, London, W1U 4EG

Reprinted 2020, 2021, 2023, 2024

British Library Cataloguing-in-Publication Data
A catalogue record for this book is available from
The British Library

Library of Congress Control Number: 2019949018

For more information, please visit *monocle.com*

MIX
Paper | Supporting
responsible forestry
FSC® C084761

This book was printed on paper certified
according to the standards of the FSC®

Edited by *Fiona Wilson, Joe Pickard*
Associate editors *Kenji Hall, Junichi Toyofuku*
Foreword by *Tyler Brûlé*

Designed by *Monocle*
Proofreading by *Monocle*
Typeset in *Plantin & Helvetica*

Printed by OGM

Printed and bound in Italy

ISBN 978-0-500-97107-9

010
Foreword

012—017
An illustrated grand tour

I.

018—138
Portrait of
a nation

A rich history, unusual topography and a culture defined by faith, beauty and tradition make Japan as enigmatic as it is enduringly appealing.

2.

140—157
Culture

From boundary-pushing modern-art museums and a thriving print scene to J-pop and karaoke, Japan consistently intrigues, informs and entertains.

142—145
Museums

146—147
Film

148—149
Media

150—151
Magazines

152
Books

153
Theatre

154—155
Music

156—157
Karaoke

3.

158—179
Design and architecture

Discover the traditional shrines and modernist masterpieces that dot Japan's skyline, as well as a few pristine residences and the iconic designs that define the nation.

160—169
Ten buildings

170—175
Residences

176—177
Design icons

178—179
Craft

4.

180—191
Transport

Japan's world-leading transport industry – from cars and trains to trams and beyond – keeps the country on a roll.

182—183
Trains

184
Bikes

185
Boats

186—187
Cars

188—189
On the street

190—191
Planes

5.

192—201
Business

Whether a small family firm or a national brand, all take pride in paying attention to detail and sharp service.

6.

202—217
Meet the people

The folk who have helped to shape Japan, from firefighters and coastguard recruits to a karate kid and a celebrity canine.

7.

218—239
Hospitality

How the island nation has refined the art of a warm welcome, whether that's in a hotel bar, tempura restaurant, family-run inn or cosy coffee shop.

220—225
Eating

226—227
What to order

228—229
Food halls

230—231
Coffee and tea

232—233
Drinking

234—239
Hotels and inns

8.

240—257
Retail

Decadent department stores, boutique businesses and impeccable customer service make shopping here an experience to remember.

242—245
Department stores

246—247
Specialists

248—249
What to buy

250—251
Fashion retailers

252—253
The art of the kimono

254—255
Grooming

256—257
Service

9.

258—291
City snapshots

From snowy Sapporo to subtropical Naha, Japan's diverse cities are friendly places to call home. Discover them through the eyes of those who know them best.

260—263
Sapporo

264—267
Tokyo

268—271
Kyoto

272—275
Osaka

276—279
Hiroshima

280—283
Fukuoka

284—287
Kagoshima

288—291
Naha

Tyler Brûlé:
A great love of Japan

When we started to plot the launch of MONOCLE way back in 2005, little did we know how big Japan's influence would be on virtually every aspect of our business. With willing investors to help get us off the ground and a host of creative contributors to shoot, illustrate and style our pages, Tokyo has been among the most prominent pins on MONOCLE's world map.

First from a bureau in Omotesando, and today from our outpost in Tomigaya, we've been committed to telling the Japan story from every angle, with our own resident editors travelling the length of the country to report on emerging businesses, ambitious artisans, forgotten villages and the sleekest new train designs. (Spool back through our past issues and you'll note that railway coverage is a main beat for our Tokyo-based colleagues).

When asked "Why the great love of Japan?" I have to think back to afternoons spent in the reading room at the Japanese Consulate in Winnipeg, Canada, age 11. I would spend hours flipping through magazines that showed glossy images of families skiing in the snowfields of Hokkaido, snappily dressed businessmen striding through the side streets of Ginza, students in smart uniforms lined-up for athletics, and department-store entrances peopled with women in felt boater-style hats and pussy bows. I wanted to learn everything I could about Japan and started tearing out stories. I even lobbied my head

teachers to renovate our school along the lines of an institution I'd spotted in Kobe. (Unsurprisingly, this was met with some laughter in the staff room and a series of detentions for spending too much time doodling other Japanese-inspired buildings and uniforms).

It took me another 10 years to finally make it to Japan and, when I got there, I found the whole experience so overwhelming that I couldn't quite absorb everything I experienced in those five days. Four years later, I returned for another short trip. Then I was back after 18 months. The following year it became a biannual affair and at the time of writing this foreword I now visit almost every month.

Whereas my visits to other cities have become routine, trips to Fukuoka, Osaka, Sapporo and Tokyo still spark within me with a sense of giddiness and anticipation. Those magazines of the 1970s filled me with a sense of wonder and it's been our ambition to do the same for you with this celebration of Japan. If you're yet to visit, we hope this volume inspires you to explore. If you've visited once or 100 times, we hope much of this serves as a reminder to all the delights Japan has to offer.

This way, please, for our tour of Japan...

An illustrated grand tour:
Jetting across Japan

Let's start in the south...

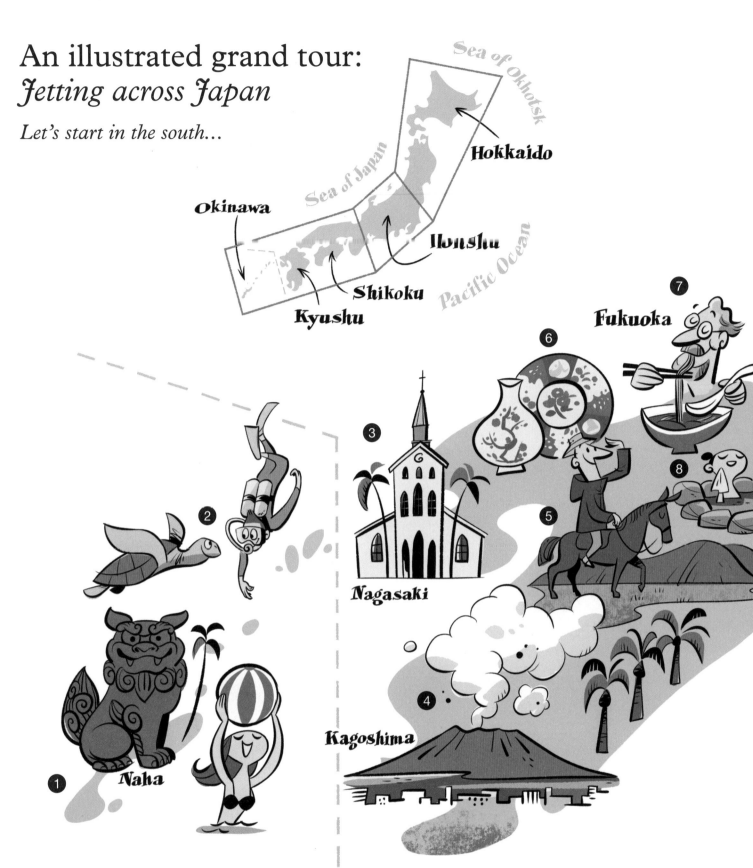

I.
Okinawa, Japan's southernmost prefecture, is spread across 150 islands ranging more than 1,000km and has long hosted US military bases.

2.
Tourists come here for the humid subtropical climate and to see turtles, rays, dugongs and colourful fish. Karate kicked off here too.

3.
Nagasaki suffered during the Second World War but the historic city has plenty to enlighten visitors. Kyushu is where Christianity arrived in 1549.

4.
Smoking occurs in some Japanese bars and restaurants. It's got nothing on Sakurajima volcano, though, which regularly puffs in public.

5.
Go see the vast caldera of Mount Aso on Kyushu island. Kuju National Park is also worth exploring: think rolling grasslands, fields and forests.

6.
Porcelain has been made in the town of Arita on Kyushu for hundreds of years. The long-coveted craft is a darling of the design world too.

7.
Creamy *tonkotsu* (pork-bone broth) ramen is a firm Fukuoka favourite. Get yours at a bustling night-time *yatai* (outdoor food stand).

8.
Kyushu has plenty of *onsen* (hot springs) at which to relax. We'd suggest trips to Beppu and Yufuin to unwind.

9.
Yamaguchi is the *fugu* (pufferfish) capital of Japan – some specialists serve it raw. Diners beware, it can be fatal if done sloppily.

10.
Izumo Taisha is an important Shinto shrine. Legend says gods and spirits meet here every year, and mortals still come to eavesdrop and find fortune.

11.
The red *torii* (traditional gate) of Itsukushima Shrine appears to float. It's a World Heritage site on Miyajima island in Hiroshima prefecture.

12.
Shikoku island is the heartland for growing citrus fruit such as yuzu and *sudachi*. Try them in a zesty condiment. Go on, don't be bitter.

13.
Island nations net a lot of fish and *katsuo* (bonito) is the signature catch at Kochi in Shikoku. *Katsuo tataki* (seared bonito) is the dish to try.

14.
Tokushima's Awa Odori dance festival is a summer hit with the nimble-footed. Elsewhere farms, forestry and fisheries provide charm.

15.
Kagawa is known for its Sanuki udon noodles. The thick, wheat-flour wonders are even marked by an Udon taxi service and mascot.

16.
Okayama prefecture is the centre of Japanese denim production and the town of Kojima has dozens of must-visit jeans shops. Just, ahem, turn up.

17.
Kobe, capital of Hyogo prefecture, is known for wagyu beef: a tender, fatty export that's tasty but pricey. Beef up the dinner budget and try it.

18.
The Tottori sand dunes are worth a gawk. Although Tottori city was decimated by an earthquake in the 1940s it's now a thriving farm region.

19.
The city of Osaka has a population of more than 2.7 million. The 16th-century castle is a marvel; the Tsutenkaku tower arrived in 1912.

20.
In Nara, Japan's capital back in the eighth century, there's plenty of ancient art, Shinto shrines, a bronze Buddha and many a roaming deer.

Moving northeast...

1.
Iga (in Mie prefecture) has a long history of teaching *ninjutsu* (ninja skills) and there's a ninja museum for the less hands-on.

2.
Kyoto was the capital of Japan until 1868 and boasts more than 1600 temples. Today the restaurant scene is worthy of a pilgrimage too.

3.
More dinosaur fossils have been found in Fukui than anywhere else in Japan. The area is also known for making paper, as well as soba noodles.

4.
Lake Biwa is a vast freshwater affair in Shiga prefecture. It's home to flora and fauna, plus plenty of secluded beaches, resorts and shrines.

5.
Japan's heavy industries are still, well, motoring. Toyota's HQ, in conveniently named Toyota City, is in Aichi prefecture. Beep beep.

6.
Shirakawa-go in Gifu prefecture is all about the *gassho-zukuri* (thatched houses) with their pitched roofs. The village is a World Heritage site.

7.
Elegant Kanazawa is known for its Edo-era architecture and has many traditional crafts to explore, including the finest decorative lacquerware.

8.
Mount Fuji – or Fuji-san as it's called in Japanese – is an active volcano and Japan's highest peak. Go on, take a hike.

9.
New leaf, anyone? Forty per cent of Japan's green tea comes from Shizuoka and the plantations date back to the 13th century. Bag it here.

10.
Atagawa Tropical & Alligator Garden is home to 140 of these snappy reptiles. For those less enamoured of gators there's a botanical garden too.

11.
Shimoda, on the Izu peninsula, is made up of mountains and sandy beaches. The scenery is beautiful and the waves are popular with surfers.

12.
Yamanashi is Japan's wine country and the nation's homegrown grape is *koshu*. The region's superb bottles are growing in esteem year on year.

13.
Rice from the coastal Niigata prefecture is rated the best in Japan by some. Decide for yourself, just don't go against the grain.

14.
Sado Island is actually a rather happy place and home to Japan's endangered *toki* (crested ibis), as well as 55,000 people.

15.
Tourists can relive the past with a ride in a *tarai bune* (bathtub boat) around Sado. The island was once a place of exile; today it's a treat.

16.
Tokyo – the sprawling, brightly lit, fast-paced capital of Japan – has a population of nearly 14 million people and counting.

17.
Tokyo Disneyland and the neighbouring DisneySea net more than 30 million visitors a year. That's taking the Mickey.

18.
Takasaki in Gunma is the birthplace of papier-mâché Daruma (wishing dolls), a symbol of perseverance and luck. Fortunate souvenirs, if you will.

19.
Utsunomiya in Tochigi has 80 shops specialising in gyoza: mouthfuls of minced meat and finely chopped vegetables in a rice-flour parcel. Yum.

20.
Tsukuba in Ibaraki prefecture is home to the Tsukuba Science City research centre and the Japan Aerospace Exploration Agency.

Heading north to Hokkaido...

1.
Thousands of flowery-hatted dancers take to the streets for the summer Hanagasa Odori festival in Tendo. The city also has hot springs.

2.
Many folksy wooden toys hail from Fukushima, including *akabeko* (a red cow) and limbless but beautiful *kokeshi* dolls. Play on.

3.
Legendary feudal lord and early Edo ruler Masamune Date was the founder of Sendai City. Visit his castle and the city's museum.

4.
Jodogahama – or Paradise Beach, as it's aptly known – is a popular spot in Iwate for a boat tour along pretty Miyako Bay.

5.
On New Year's Eve in the Akita city of Oga, adults dress as *namahage* (demons) to warn children about laziness. A good idea, if you ask us.

6.
Fifty different varieties and nearly half a million tonnes of apples – half of Japan's total – hail from Aomori. A core industy indeed.

7.
The town of Oma in Aomori is famous for its plump, sometimes hatchback-sized, *hon-maguro* (blue-fin tuna). Scale is everything here.

8.
Ski resort Niseko has an average snowfall of eight metres a year. Skiers come from all around the world for the deep powder.

Sendai

There's plenty more to explore...

Sapporo

9.
Sapporo, the capital of Hokkaido, only joined Japan in the 1870s. Today it's home to a fishmarket and fleets that ply nearby northern waters.

10.
Most of Japan's thoroughbred horses come from Hidaka in Hokkaido, while close-by Mount Chiroro is a hit with hikers and climbers.

11.
Wheat has been grown in Hokkaido for 50 years, much of it in Tokachi. You'll also see dairy farms, vineyards, cornfields and lavender.

12.
Hokkaido is Japan's big sky country, with volcanoes, vast open spaces and a sizeable population of large brown bears.

13.
Tsurui-Ito Tancho Sanctuary safeguards the red-crowned crane. It was established in 1987 to protect the birds and their wetland habitat.

1

一

Portrait of a nation
ニッポン

On a map of the world, Japan appears like a mark in ink. It's fitting that this slender archipelago – stretching for some 3,000km across four main islands, or almost 7,000 in total – assumes the form of calligraphy. In Japan, there is always the aspiration of something finer.

The country is perennially a-dance with topography: three-quarters of it is mountain, peppered with volcanic exclamation marks; inland seas foster unusual flora and fauna; dense forests rise out of morning mists, stunning in their seasonal distinction. To see the scale from the top of a tower in Tokyo takes the breath clean away; at street level, nowhere can match the density and detail.

In the mid-17th century, Japan removed itself from trade and relations with the world for more than 200 years; the country grew accustomed to doing its own thing, developing a culture defined by beauty, tradition, precision and dedication. In recent years, fascinated voyeurs have gawped at its pop culture and architecture, its extraordinary food and dogged pursuit of perfection. Until recently, Japan met that fascination with polite bafflement, never quite understanding why others were so interested. But contemporary Japan is an outward-looking nation, engaging more than ever.

Everywhere is different to somewhere but Japan is unique. Here are the elements that we think make this enigmatic country so enduringly appealing.

Tradition:
In with the old

In Japan, tradition and modernity coexist comfortably. The country has some magnificent ancient buildings and yet history doesn't always come in old garb. Japanese cities have been transformed by bombs, earthquakes and postwar development but scratch the surface and the old ways are still very much in place. A concrete building might well house a centuries-old business while a modern ryokan will happily borrow its style of hospitality from traditional establishments that have been run the same way for generations. This is a country that celebrates its cultural heritage in everything from food and fashion to craft and design but is never afraid of an update.

Japan is filled with hidden treasures, including Mameshin, a family-run *ryotei* (restaurant) that has been in business in the city of Otsu for more than a century. It offers regional dishes such as *funazushi* (fermented sushi) made with fish caught in nearby Lake Biwa.

Myogon-in, a sub-temple in the grounds of Miidera, has been converted into lodgings.

The lodgings that look to the future while borrowing from the past

Traditional buildings have a big role to play in modern hospitality in Japan, with travellers continuing to enjoy the simple pleasures of tatami mats, sliding screens and a futon mattress. Japanese temples have a long tradition of offering trainee monks and pilgrims a place to rest for the night. These humble lodgings are known as *shukubo*. The 1,300-year-old Buddhist temple of Miidera, at the foot of Mount Hiei, houses one of the more luxurious examples. It has dozens of historical wooden buildings in its sprawling grounds and in 2018 one of its sub-temples opened as lodgings for paying guests.

Hakone Retreat Före has historical buildings in its grounds.

Onsen (hot springs) are at the heart of Japan's bathing culture. These baths use water heated by volcanic activity in the Earth's crust.

Hakone Retreat Före is set deep within
the forest. Its cypress-wood *onsen*
is popular with guests who come to
soak in the silky water, which is rich
in calcium and magnesium.

When the Hotel Okura in Tokyo reopened after a major rebuild in 2019, guests were happy to see the return of the lift attendants in full kimono greeting guests as they had done in the old hotel.

Koichiro Aoki is general manager at
the Hotel New Grand in Yokohama.
This European-style hotel was built
in 1927 and its old-school grandeur
still attracts a steady stream of
architecture buffs.

The individuals who have long been honing their craft

Japan is full of master craftspeople, traditional stage artists and virtuoso musicians. The most accomplished practitioners, who have been perfecting their crafts for decades, are rewarded with the accolade of "Living National Treasure". While many play a vital role in preserving unique techniques and performance styles that might be hundreds of years old, these are not the stuffy standard-bearers of traditional culture. In fact, it would be hard to meet a more spirited, open-minded collection of people. They've seen it all: war and postwar hardship, natural disasters and economic boom and bust. And all the while they've continued diligently to pursue their crafts.

Embroiderer Kiju Fukuda was a Living National Treasure since 1997. His silk kimonos are decorated with motifs drawn from nature and realised with such skill and vitality as to appear three-dimensional.

Koto player Shoin Yamase still lives in the house where she grew up. Her musical endeavours started young when she learned to dance, sing and play both the shamisen (a three-stringed instrument) and the koto, the 13-stringed instrument for which her mother's family was known.

The ceremony that has come to define Japanese culture

Japan has a number of traditional arts that have survived over the centuries. The addition of the suffix "*do*" has come to indicate a practice or "way": *kado* (flowers), *shodo* (calligraphy), *kodo* (incense) and judo (which simply means the "gentle" way). The way of tea is known as *sado* (or *chado*) and for many is the most distilled essence of Japanese culture. The tea ceremony is a carefully choreographed assemblage of elements: traditional architecture, tea bowls and a scroll hanging from the wall, perfectly judged to match the day or season. Powdered green tea is whisked and served with some *wagashi* (traditional Japanese confectionery) by the practitioner, whose precise motions are learned and internalised over many years so as to appear quite natural. There are several schools of tea, the most famous descended from 16th-century tea master Sen no Rikyu.

The decades-old coffee shops that continue to bring people together
People think of Japan as a tea-drinking country but it's also one of the biggest consumers of coffee in the world – the Japanese have been drinking the stuff since missionaries and traders arrived with it in the 17th century. Central to this growth has been the *kissaten* (coffee shop), which evolved as Japan started to urbanise at the end of the 19th century.

Today there are more than 67,000 *kissaten* across the country, ranging from smoky station pit-stops to specialist affairs where the master precision-brews each cup. There are jazz *kissa*, literary *bungaku* cafés lined with books and *meikyoku kissa* (classical music cafés where listening to music is the purpose and talking is frowned upon). The *kissaten* has always offered a democratic space: for some they are a refuge from the obligations of daily life; for others they offer company, conversation and community.

This page: Lawn in Yotsuya, Tokyo, opened in 1968. Opposite: nestled among the antiquarian bookshops and publishing houses of Jinbocho is Ladrio. Opened in 1949, this café was the first in downtown Tokyo to serve Vienna coffee topped with Chantilly cream.

The traditional *kissaten* menu features a medley of western dishes that, like coffee, Japan has made its own. The staples are sandwiches – particularly *tamago-sando* (egg sandwiches) – and thick white toast, usually part of the "morning set" breakfast menu. Some also offer an old-school "Napolitan" tomato spaghetti or an *omuraisu* (rice-filled omelette).

Kissaten owners know they can't compete with chains on price and they don't want to be compared. They pride themselves on offering a different service, complete with wet hand towels and refills of iced water.

The drinks list generally includes
a milkshake – the classic *kissaten*
version is a whisked mix of raw egg,
milk and sugar – and a melon float
(a scoop of ice cream atop a lime-
green fizzy drink).

Kissaten numbers may have dwindled
but there's still an older clientele who
appreciate what a long-established
coffee shop can offer, as well as a
younger audience keen to learn.

Camelback in Tokyo's Tomigaya neighbourhood is worth a stop not just for a coffee poured by Keitaro Suzuki (*pictured, far right*); the slender stand also has the added attraction of Hayato Naruse's sandwiches. A former sushi chef, Naruse (*pictured, far left*) applies the same precision and technique to the humble sandwich, elevating it to something special; his *tamago-sando* (egg sandwich) is a glorious update of the *kissaten* classic.

The cafés creating new traditions with beans sourced from afar

In Japan's modern café scene, young owners brimming with new ideas have made being a barista a popular profession. These small independents appeal to customers with a quality-over-quantity philosophy, running micro roasters and making perfect cappuccinos and hand-brewed cups of coffee from beans grown on sunny slopes in Ethiopia and Honduras.

Young, independent cafés such as Fuglen (*this page*) and Nem (*opposite, top right*) in Tokyo are opening all over Japan, with an emphasis on good interior design and a modern food menu.

Nature:
The great outdoors

Don't be fooled by images of Tokyo's sprawl; Japan is a nature-rich island nation. Nearly 70 per cent of the land is covered with woodland and there are thousands of lakes, rivers and mountain peaks. The 3,000km-long archipelago has a diverse climate that ranges from subarctic Hokkaido to subtropical Okinawa, which is home to wildlife such as the Iriomote wildcat and sea eagles. Everything from forestry to fishing revolves around the four seasons, and punishing typhoons and earthquakes have taught the people the art of respecting and living with nature.

The outdoor pursuit that's keeping the nation fit and healthy
Wherever you are in Japan, mountain ranges big and small loom on the horizon. Unsurprisingly, such a landscape has inspired the country's residents to become world-class mountaineers and mountaineering photographers, who conquer international peaks such as Mount Everest and K2. For the ordinary, however, climbing Mount Fuji – Japan's tallest peak – is a common goal. Mountain Day is a national holiday that takes place each year on 11 August and sees enthusiasts and outdoor types embark on hiking routes around local mountains nationwide. And it's done in style: both young and old don special hiking gear for the occasion.

From April to November, the popular Tateyama–Kurobe Alpine Route connects Tateyama to Ogizawa via a sacred mountain, hydroelectric dam and boiling-hot spring (all accompanied with a hearty dose of dramatic scenery).

Deep in Japan's Northern Alps, the Tateyama-Kurobe Alpine Route stretches across a 37km-long mountain range that encompasses more than 70 peaks.

Buddhist monks were scaling peaks as early as the 8th century, preaching reverence for the mountains and building temples. At Oyama-jinja shrine atop Mount Tateyama, a Shinto priest purifies worshippers.

The rural pockets of Japan that make their own rules
The Japanese countryside is blessed with fertile farmland and ancient forests, as well as rich traditions and local cultures that have been handed down from generation to generation over the centuries. There are also myriad dialects: each of the 47 prefectures of Japan has its own unique accents, words and expressions. With arguably the world's best transport system, most places in Japan are a swift Shinkansen ride away. But there are still plenty of remote areas nestled in green valleys and at the end of winding paths – and that's where you might just find the most charming people.

Shirakawa-go is a small village in Gifu prefecture known for its perfectly preserved *gassho-zukuri* (tall timber homes with triangular, thatched roofs).

The manmade creations that explore the bond between people and nature
To understand Japan's gardens is to understand the relationship between its people and the natural environment. The *karesansui* (dry landscape) at Ryoan-ji and Daitoku-ji temples in Kyoto reflect the influences of Zen, which took root in Japan in the 13th century, while the 17th-century Shugakuin Imperial Villa uses the *shakkei* method of incorporating background views into the composition. Developed over centuries, Japanese gardens vary in size and style – but all tell stories about how the people interpret the country's natural landscape. Unsurprisingly, those who create them require a vast bank of knowledge.

The Adachi Museum of Art in Yasugi, a city on the north coast of central Japan, is home to one of the country's most famous gardens. The museum's founder, Zenko Adachi, believed that a garden should be regarded as a living painting.

The White Gravel and Pine Garden
at the Adachi Museum of Art was
designed as a tribute to the painter
Taikan Yokoyama.

Landscape designer Mirei Shigemori
created about 200 gardens for
temples, shrines and private homes
in the 20th century. Chequerboard
moss-and-stone patterns are a feature
of his work.

Japanese gardens are refined
distillations of the natural world.
They reflect the changing seasons,
symbolise mythical places in miniature
and often provide a sublime backdrop
to traditional wooden buildings.

Bonsai is thought to have arrived from China centuries ago. Its modern practitioners run apprenticeships, seminars and conventions, and have both an artistic eye and a botanist's green thumb.

The planting method that has perfected the art of miniature trees

Bonsai (literally "tray planting") is a unique type of gardening where trees are planted in small trays or pots and carefully snipped, pruned, root trimmed and trained to grow perfectly in miniature and evoke a full-scale tree. The best place to see this in action is Omiya Bonsai Village in Saitama, just outside Tokyo. A group of professional bonsai gardeners moved there from Tokyo after the Great Kanto Earthquake of 1923 and established the village two years later. There were a few rules for residency, including limitations on the height of houses (to avoid disrupting the scenery) and the ownership of at least 10 bonsai trees. Today there is also a museum that explores the full history of bonsai and has 70-odd trees on display. Several gardens are also open to the public, including Mansei-en, owned by the Kato family who have been cultivating bonsai for five generations. Their collection includes a Japanese juniper that's more than 1,000 years old.

Faith:
Beyond belief

Religion plays a curiously ambiguous role in Japanese society. People line up in their millions to pray for good health and fortune at Shinto shrines at New Year, get married in faux Christian chapels and observe Buddhist funeral rites. Shinto is the native religion and its influence is pervasive even in secular Japan. It identifies spirits in nature and embraces myriad folk beliefs; it's easy to spot a shrine by its *torii* (traditional gate). Buddhism came to Japan later, via China and Korea in the sixth century, but sits alongside Shinto as one of the country's two main religions.

The belief system that's been with Japan from the beginning
Shinto identifies *kami* (spirits and deities) all around. Despite having no founder, sacred scriptures or fixed dogmas, its guiding beliefs have remained intact for centuries. People will often stop at a shrine to pray; it's also where many choose to get married and where children dress in traditional clothes for their *Shichi-go-san* (seven-five-three) ceremony, a rite of passage. Before praying, worshippers cleanse themselves by ladling water over their hands.

Up and down Japan, *matsuri* (festivals) are marked by walking through the streets carrying a *mikoshi* (portable shrine) that's used to transport a deity. In the summer months *mikoshi* can be seen all over Japan; even if you can't spy the action, you'll hear the distinctive shouts of the carriers. This particular *mikoshi* is part of the Karato autumn festival on the island of Teshima.

056

Saké barrels on display at a Shinto shrine. Although these barrels – known as *kazaridaru* – are merely decorative, they are significant since saké is drunk at shrines and religious festivals. Several shrines are even licensed to make their own.

The religion that's all about renewal
Buddhism offers a spiritual path involving an endless cycle of birth, death and rebirth. Release from this continuum can only be achieved by following in the footsteps of the Buddha and becoming enlightened, a transcendent state free from hatred and greed. Today roughly 70 per cent of Japan's population consider themselves Buddhist.

In 2015, Pritzker Prize-winning architect Tadao Ando created the "Hill of the Buddha", an artificial hill planted with lavender that partially envelops a 13.5-metre-high statue of Buddha at Makomanai Takino Cemetery in Sapporo. The whole statue can only be seen by those who walk through a 135-metre-long approach and look up; from a distance only the top of the head is visible.

Sport:
Head in the game

Japan is a sports-mad nation. School children are encouraged to pick a sport – from kendo and judo to baseball, football and basketball – and train physically and mentally. The spirit of never-give-up and teamwork are fostered from a young age. Many people continue to play as adults (after-work futsal on the rooftop or Sunday baseball) and pass on the passion to their own children. Stadiums are full of spectators young and old, who faithfully cheer on their teams; win or lose, Japanese fans give it their all.

The sport that keeps spectators glued to their seats and screens
First brought over from the US in 1872, baseball is now the biggest sport in Japan. It's a national pastime; there is a professional league of 12 teams with keen fans from Hokkaido to Kyushu. Top players make more than ¥540m (€4.5m) a year. Megastars, who make it to Major League Baseball in the US, can expect even more astronomical salaries and a constant entourage of Japanese journalists. Every summer, youngsters at 4,000 high schools compete for the national championship, Koshien, which has an equally avid following.

Fans of the Hanshin Tigers, who hail from Osaka and Hyogo prefectures and other nearby regions, plan their lives around games. They also display their devotion in typical outlandish fashion: striped tails, tiger masks and custom-made, elaborately embroidered outfits.

As the latecomers find their seats at the Tigers' home stadium, Koshien, *uriko* – young women in clashing pink, red and orange outfits and knee-high socks – roam the aisles carrying 20kg kegs of beer in search of thirsty spectators: a full crowd will gulp down some 30,000 cups.

The sport that's more than a sport
Legend has it that the very origins of
Japan depended on the outcome of a sumo
match. The archipelago was supposedly
ceded to the Japanese when their leader,
the god Takemikazuchi, out-wrestled the
leader of a rival people. The first matches
were Shinto rituals dedicated to the gods
and the sport flourished under Imperial
patronage. Sumo's connection with Shinto
is still an integral part of the sport: the roof
that hangs over the *dohyo* (ring) resembles
a Shinto shrine; the black gauze hats worn
by the referees are modelled after those
of Shinto priests; and when a wrestler
steps into the ring (which, incidentally, no
woman is permitted to do), he purifies it
symbolically by throwing salt in the air.

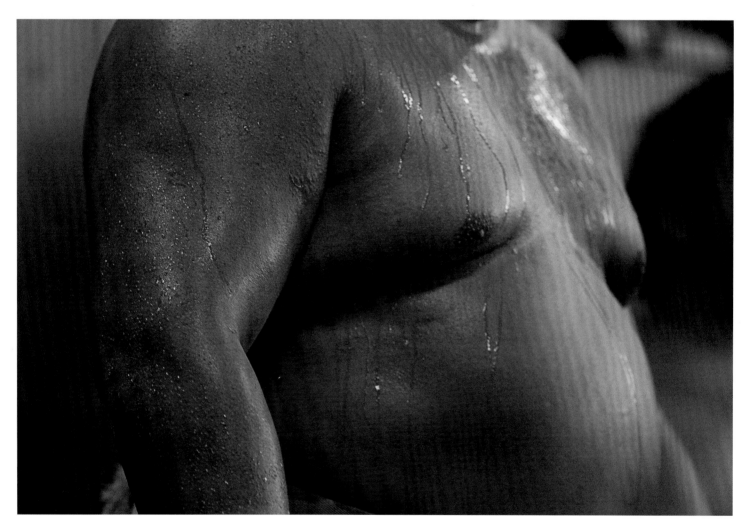

A wrestler's daily routine is a repetitive regimen: training, eating, sleeping, then more training. The wrestlers sleep in a shared room and train, cook and eat together. Only when he reaches a certain rank can a wrestler have his own room or live outside the stable.

A tournament lasts for 15 days, with each *rikishi* (wrestler) fighting a different opponent from their division each day. The individual with the highest number of wins becomes the tournament champion.

Spaces:
Master plans

Japan is a living museum of architecture old and new. *Miyadaiku* (temple and shrine carpenters) are keeping centuries-old building techniques and know-how alive while award-winning architects are designing cutting-edge spaces in which people want to live and work in the city and the countryside. Design and craftsmanship go hand in hand. Behind each big-name architect is a team of craftspeople and construction workers who make their designs possible, whether that's with intricate *kumiko* wooden screens or silky-smooth concrete walls. Tokyo is paving the way when it comes to finding solutions to compact urban living but Japan's architectural gems exist beyond the capital. The country is filled with structures, both world-renowned and anonymous, that range from modernist housing blocks to traditional wooden farmhouses.

Inside Kagawa Prefectural Budokan, a 1966 martial-arts venue that's a concrete interpretation of traditional wooden carpentry.

Contemporary urban houses are often
built on tiny plots of land that make
creative use of the small dimensions
to maximise sunlight and incorporate
features such as a parking space.

071

Japan's shrines and temples are places of worship and protectors of the country's architectural heritage. They're privately run but often fulfil an important public role. They are the social glue for neighbourhoods and communities, hosting local festivals and farmers' markets, and acting as venues for weddings, funerals and meditation retreats.

Japan's farmhouses and *machiya* (traditional townhouses) are widely admired as historical landmarks. They're also a source of inspiration for a younger generation of architects whose projects offer modern versions of *doma* (pressed-earth entrances) and sunlit *engawa* (terraces).

With their *shoji* (paper screens), ceramic roof tiles and exposed beams, Japan's century-old wooden shops and houses are elegant, austere and practical. Thin wooden slats let air pass through while shielding the interior from prying eyes.

Ichinomiya Danchi, a housing complex designed by modernist master Kenzo Tange, draws architecture buffs from around the country to the southwestern city of Takamatsu.

At first glance, Japanese cities may appear to be sterile and grey but look closer and you'll discover cobblestone streets and narrow alleyways weaving their way behind modern buildings and broad boulevards. Greenery sprouts in the smallest of spaces, adding splashes of colour to residential façades and pavements.

The hotel that was destroyed and then brought back to life

When the main wing of the Hotel Okura in Tokyo was demolished in 2015 there was a lingering sense of loss at the disappearance of an irreplaceable slice of Japanese modernism. Created in 1962 by the architect Yoshiro Taniguchi, with the help of an exceptional group of artists and craftspeople, the Okura's peerless sense of time and place peaked with the famous lobby, a space so atmospheric that its power remained undimmed 50 years on. To idle in the airy lobby or sip a cocktail in the smoky Orchid Bar was to wallow in a Tokyo that is fast disappearing. In 2019 the hotel reopened inside a gleaming new skyscraper, and the much-loved lobby was perfectly, confoundingly, recreated. For those familiar with the original, walking into the Heritage wing of the new Okura Tokyo is disconcerting. The iconic lounge chairs, lacquer tables, pendant lights and woven hangings are all there. The vintage time zone map of the world is in place; even the bamboo shadows peep through the paper screens as they once did. The top-to-bottom remake took years and demanded a hardworking team of craftspeople from all over Japan.

Mobility:
On the move

Efficiency and speed are the standard hallmarks of progress. That's true in Japan but it's not the only measure. Service is an important part of engaging with customers, and the country's fleet of taxis and high-speed trains are where you'll find some of the transport industry's most thoroughly attentive staff. This is a nation that really knows how to get people comfortably from A to B – and not a minute late.

The train line that turned two faraway cities into easy-to-reach destinations
When the new Hokuriku Shinkansen line opened in March 2015, it connected Tokyo directly to two cities that had been previously hard to reach: Kanazawa and Toyama. A half-century in the making, the line was conceived as a back-door channel between Tokyo and Osaka that would keep commerce humming if an earthquake or tsunami were to disrupt travel along the Pacific coastline. Even in a country with thousands of kilometres of high-speed rail track, the new line had an instant impact. It bridged the gap between Japan's commercial centre and a far-flung region, boosting tourism, business and investment.

081

The soft-power driving forces rolling up and down Japan's streets

Japan's taxi operators make it their mission to provide impeccable service. Interiors are pristine and seats even have embroidered covers. Drivers wear white gloves and are deferential and polite; they have hydraulic levers to open and close the back door for customers. In many ways taxis are a roaming brigade of soft-power ambassadors, reinforcing Japan's already-stellar reputation for hospitality.

In 1912, the first taxis (six Ford Model T cars) appeared on the streets of Tokyo. Today the city has 44,000 taxis, triple the number of yellow cabs in New York.

You often find uniformed security guards standing around construction sites, car parks and crowded train stations in Japan's big cities. But in a country with a low crime rate, these guards keep themselves busy with other tasks such as sweeping up debris, directing traffic and apologising to passers-by for inconveniences.

The airport that leaves all other hubs standing

Tokyo's Haneda Airport opened its new international terminal in 2010 with an Edo-period-inspired shopping village – and the concept still looks as fresh as the day it was launched. An abundance of timber and intricate details lends warmth to the cavernous glass-and-steel terminal. Add to that the all-star roster of Japanese tenants – selling everything from tea and stationery to books and skincare – and you have a winning combination that beats the predictable look of most major city airports.

The retail centrepiece of the departure building is the fourth-floor Edo Koji, an extraordinary take on a historical Japanese town by master craftsman Yoshiaki Nakamura.

Urbanism:
Life in the city

Japan's urban landscape is
a patchwork of conflicting
interests: the grand and well-
funded butting up against the
small-scale and grass-roots.
Navigating this is what city
life is all about. There's beauty
in the organic and accidental;
a hypermodern building
sitting next to an old temple.
City-planners would prefer
to commission elaborate
blueprints and fund vast clean-
ups than regenerate entire
neighbourhoods over years
– but there's a lot that can't
be plotted out. Sometimes
the public finds uses for
open spaces, purpose-built
structures and small gaps that
no municipal official sitting at
a desk could have dreamed of.
It's messy but this chaos – this
possibility of the unexpected
– is what energises a city and
its residents.

**The urban projects doing things a
little differently**
All streets benefit from a flourish of greenery
and Koen Dori (appropriately, Park Street)
in Tokyo's busy Shibuya district is particularly
leafy. Since 2008 the local shop association
has hosted an annual flower festival during
the Golden Week holiday in spring, and
there has also been a gardening contest that
opened up drab patches between road and
pavement to 23 professional gardeners from
across Japan. The association stumps up
the cost and passers-by can enjoy the mini
gardens for a year. It's a lesson to share –
taking a collective approach to softening a
city's edges and adding some welcome green.

Viewed from overhead, the Air Track in Osaka is a rather perplexing sight: a 300-metre-long running track raised above a dense urban neighbourhood. The development also has a climbing wall and a fitness centre with a swimming pool, as well as healthcare clinics, a smart library and shops including a pharmacy, florist and dry cleaner.

Japan's oldest amusement park, Hanayashiki, opened in 1853 as a flower park. It's now a tightly packed collection of rides and other attractions hemmed in on all sides by the low-rise neighbourhood of Tokyo's Asakusa district. The roller coaster, built in 1953, reaches a speed of 42km/h.

本醸造酒・純米酒

The ubiquitous machines that keep customers satisfied and sated

Japan has upwards of 4.2 million vending machines – one for every 30 citizens, the highest per capita in the world. Most sell drinks but others run the gamut: newspapers, cigarettes, toys, stamps, batteries, business cards, novels, undergarments, hot dogs, apple slices, frozen dumplings, lipstick and condoms. Sales from vending machines exceed ¥4.7trn (€38bn) annually. The vending machine has a special place in the national psyche; it embodies Japan's love of gadgets. They're everywhere you look – on street corners, at train stations and even atop Mount Fuji.

On the east side of the Japanese capital, retailer Tokyo Shouten's vending machine experiment has been a hit. Three machines at the back of the shop pour small cups of saké from 30 different chilled bottles.

The food stalls bringing the flavours of Japan out onto the street

There's joy in the thought of tucking into food made at a stall, cart or truck. First, the simplicity: no utensils or ambience – just the flavours of the thing you've been handed. In Japan, street food is summer-festival fare from *yatai* (outdoor food stands): pork-seafood-cabbage *okonomiyaki* (pancakes), *takoyaki* (octopus balls), pan-fried yakisoba noodles, grilled corn on a stick and candy floss. It's the sweet potato baked in a wood-fire stove in a mini-truck in Tokyo; the *kara-age* (deep-fried) chicken made in a cubby-hole space with a window in Osaka; and the bowl of ramen cooked in the pot on a rickety, old wooden cart on the pavement in Fukuoka. It's where chefs start off small and the late-night crowd know they'll find nourishment.

At Densuke Shoten, in the city of Naha on the southern island of Okinawa, diners enjoy sashimi, ox tongue and pork stew. It's what is known as a *sen-bero*, a hole-in-the-wall restaurant where you can get tipsy for a mere ¥1,000 (€8).

While residents in other countries might prefer to zip up a raincoat in a light shower, Japan's city-dwellers typically reach for their umbrellas. It's no wonder the Japanese buy more than 130 million umbrellas a year. It's also the reason unclaimed umbrellas account for more than 30 per cent of all misplaced possessions.

**The community policing that's kept
Japan's streets safe since the 1870s**
When it comes to keeping the peace, Japan's
cities have a tried-and-tested solution that's
been in place for 150 years. On street corners
along busy roads, *koban* (police boxes) are
staffed around the clock by officers who
give directions, return lost wallets and
occasionally chase after law-breakers.

In cities across Japan, the tearing
down and rebuilding seems to have no
end. The workers at construction sites
are easy to pick out: their preferred
look includes hard hats, utility belts
and flared trousers.

In every park, temple or shrine, a crew of hard-working gardeners trim the grass, sweep the paths, rake the leaves and keep everything looking extraordinarily tidy.

Along Japan's roadways, steel-and-concrete pedestrian bridges arch overhead. These sturdy elevated walkways – nearly 11,500 in 2018 – first appeared in the 1960s and 1970s and are a symbol of the country's rapid motorisation and the concerns about pedestrian safety. Usually painted sky blue, the footbridges stand in lieu of zebra crossings.

渋谷区神園町

The pockets of green carving out open spaces in Japan's densely packed cities
From high above Japan's city streets, you can spot the patches of greenery. They might be wooded parks or the manicured gardens of temples and shrines. Amid the concrete and asphalt, these slices of nature act as a buffer against the summer heat and make the nation's cities more pleasant to live in. They're habitats for wildlife, social gathering spots for communities and open-air spaces for residents (who tend to live in tiny dwellings) to escape to – whether they want to tan, play music, dance or kick a ball around.

In the concrete jungle, parks – such as this one in Sapporo – are a visual reminder of the seasons. During cherry-blossom season in spring and peak leaf-viewing in autumn, Japan's city parks attract hordes of families, young couples and seniors who are there to take in the view.

Shinjuku Gyoen, a garden in Tokyo,
offers manicured lawns and trimmed
trees just a short walk from the
world's busiest train station.

Parks in Japan are made for everything
from running and yoga to napping.
They're a good place to spar with
a karate partner and you can shout
without worrying too much about a
backlash from neighbours.

There are 50,000 plants – and 120 varieties – in the rooftop garden of ACROS Fukuoka, a cultural facility in the centre of the city. Also known as the Step Garden, it allows greenery to pour down the side of the building and has become a city landmark. The garden is open to the public, who can also enjoy the view from the park below.

Children:
Room to grow

Children in Japan walk to and from school by themselves, either along empty lanes in the country or through chock-a-block Shinjuku Station in Tokyo. It's just safe. Most pupils go to the nearest public schools, sharing a uniform experience with their peers in the neighbourhood. The world's healthiest, and perhaps tastiest, lunch is served and discipline is taught through a range of subjects and sports. Parks are open to all and friendly neighbours keep their watchful eyes on them. And ticking over in the background, both at home and in the classroom, are years and years spent learning one of the world's most difficult languages.

The new and improved nurseries catering to every child's needs
Most newly built nurseries, pre-schools and daycare centres in Japan stick to a predictable design template: long, straight corridors, boxy rooms and too many fluorescent bulbs. They are easy to clean and they do a good job of fulfilling administrators' needs – but less so those of the children who use them. Three smart nurseries located on the southwestern island of Kyushu – Obama Kodomoen (*pictured*), Akune Megumi Kindergarten and Daiichi Kindergarten – are setting a new standard. Laid out with wooden floors, tiny spaces that children find comforting and plenty of natural light, they also feature an array of indoor slides, climbing nets and monkey bars.

Obama Kodomoen is a two-storey building overlooking Tachibana Bay. The operator, a temple in Unzen city, had mentioned concerns to Taku Hibino – head of Hibino Sekkei Architecture – about idle, overweight children. As a result, Hibino made a slide next to the stairs, as well as nets and a pole for children to hoist and lower themselves between floors.

The community centre educating children about food

In a residential area behind Tokyo's busy Ebisu Station, Kageoka no Ie (House in Kageoka) is a non-profit community centre funded by public money but run by the private sector. "Everyone is welcome here," says director Kisako Omi. "Parents with toddlers, schoolchildren, teenagers and the elderly." There was a house on this plot of land but when the owner died in 1998 the property was donated to Shibuya City Social Welfare Council. The council ran it as a community meeting place but it never took off due to its clunky layout. Now it's used for numerous purposes but food is the central theme. "We take *shoku-iku* [food education] very seriously," says Omi. "Food plays such a critical role in raising children. It nurtures not only our body but also our heart."

Work:
The daily grind

Why does everything run like clockwork in Japan? Perhaps because the nation is powered by some of the hardest-working people in the world. Services are carried out with military precision: public transport shuttles millions to work on time, bike messengers fly around the city, and printing services dash out business cards and presentations. There are also more women in the workplace than ever before. And yes, delicious lunch spots (izakaya pubs included) are also no doubt key to Japan's world of work being such a success.

The people working from dawn until dusk and beyond

Dressed in a suit and a tie, often with a company pin in their lapel, salary men come straight out of high school or university into a world of strict rules and hierarchies. They are pitied but also admired for their hard work; they are the backbone of the world's third-largest economy. They may snooze on the train (or collapse outside the stations on a Friday night) but there is a thing or two the world can learn from their unparalleled professional work ethic. Salary men share a strong sense of collective responsibility and goals. Traditionally, many devoted their lives to a single company but today careers are more fragmented. The government is doing its bit to alleviate fatigue by passing laws to limit overtime and force tired workers to use their holiday allowance. These days, after a brief stint, some entrepreneurial young workers are ditching corporate life altogether and setting up their own companies.

The counters of izakaya, noodle houses and speciality restaurants are where you'll find the nation's office workers after hours. Here they wind down with colleagues, drain glasses of beer and share plates of food to nourish themselves for the next day's battle.

There are strict rules when it comes to doing business in Japan: you must be punctual, polite and dress the part. It doesn't matter whether you're in a senior position or the new recruit, and often it's the veterans in the room who set the best example.

BELL CAPTAIN

The exercises that most of Japan's residents wake up to every morning
To millions of Japanese, mornings wouldn't be the same without *rajio taiso* (radio exercises). Nearly everyone knows the five-minute *dai-ichi* (first) routine by heart. From very early on they learn the moves at school or in neighbourhood parks and commit to memory the soundtrack that public broadcaster NHK airs on TV and radio up to seven times a day. When they join the workforce it's often a part of their daily regime, whether in an office, a shop or a factory.

At the Mitsubishi Electric global headquarters in Tokyo, nearly everyone in the factory automation-systems group gets up for the five-minute morning session.

At Meiji's milk-and-yoghurt factory in Toda city, north of Tokyo, the *rajio taiso* theme song marks the start of the day. Lasting just five minutes, the exercises are a crucial warm-up for employees before they head to their stations.

Seniors:
Full of years

Japan is facing the twin demographic challenge of a low birth rate and an increasingly elderly population. Current predictions are that by 2040, 35 per cent of the population of Japan will be over 65. The fact that Japanese seniors are living longer than ever is prompting discussions about raising the national retirement age. They impress with their *ikigai* (zest for life) and have plenty to offer the community; magazines and fashion brands are increasingly catering to their interests. The future make-up of the population is shaping government policy – and where Japan leads, other countries will follow.

Japanese seniors are as fit and active as their children. They have plenty of hobbies – from pottery and gardening to tennis classes – and they practise them all in style.

129

Spry retirees keep themselves
engaged with the latest news
around the world. They bike to
their neighbourhood libraries
to read, get together and perhaps
play *shogi* (Japanese chess).

Idiosyncrasies:
Go your own way

Living in a country with a low crime rate and high standard of living has its perks – not least the luxury of spending time and disposable income in unusual ways. Domestic tourists fly across the country to attend mascot beauty contests and dog owners pamper their pets like children, with trips to salons and excursions with the pooch seated in a high-end pram.

The corporate mascots that inhabit a central part of the nation's identity
Yuru-kyara (loose characters) – the large, cuddly and sometimes offbeat mascots now omnipresent in Japan – have become part of the PR strategy for every municipality, government agency, industry association and snack-maker. There are even smiling mascots for prisons. The characters act like celebrities, reaching out to fans through websites, blogs and social media, announcing where and when their next gig will be and making it look as if they lead lives just like everyone else. They attract tourists to remote towns, raise awareness about little-known causes and present a loveable face for companies, organisations and lock-up facilities that could use one. Like celebrities, they also have an image to maintain. Diehard *yuru-kyara* fans will insist that there's nobody inside the suit.

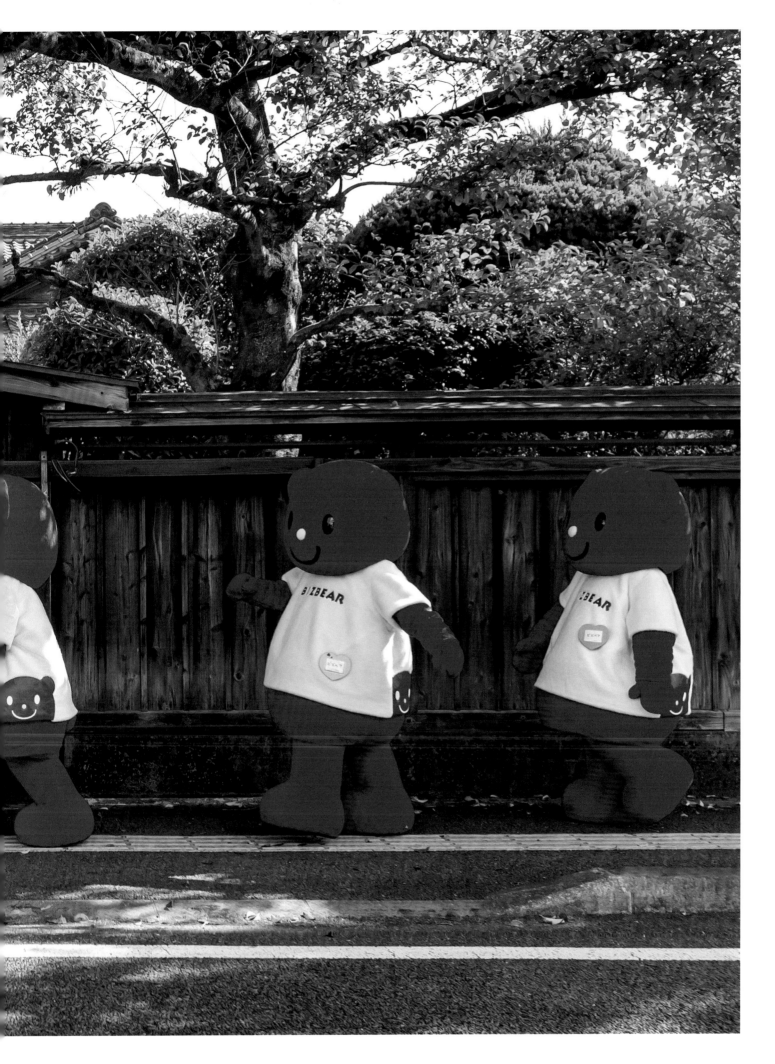

Muu-chan is one of Miyazaki prefecture's trio of canine mascots (Hii-kun and Kaa-kun are the other two). Since 2011, they have appeared at events and done wonders for tourism and trade in this southwestern region of nearly 1.1 million residents.

Kigurumi.biz's factory in Miyazaki is where Japan's best-known mascot stars are carved, glued and stitched together – then photographed like film stars. No, sorry, they're not real.

Japan is a dog-loving country with just under nine million canines. Tokyo's streets are teeming with pert chihuahuas and miniature schnauzers dressed to the nines and lounging in dog buggies.

There are thousands of pet salons
in Japan, offering everything from an
old-school trim and fluffy blow-out
to avant-garde styling.

Tokyo's Yoyogi Park is one of the city's most popular spots for dog walkers. For those who don't have their own, there are businesses nearby where customers can pay to borrow a canine companion.

2
二

Culture
文化

Japan's unique culture has captivated visitors for centuries. The Meiji restoration first opened the diverse nation's treasure trove of delights to the wider world in the 19th century but Japan still has secrets, successes and intrigues that the rest of us are just waking up to.

There's more than geisha girls, Harajuku hairdos and manga to manage. Here we see how envelope-pushing modern-art museums exist alongside institutions dedicated to keeping craft alive. We peruse bookshops that are writing the next chapter in global retail, visit beachside cinemas we would like to see take root elsewhere, and peek inside animation studios that export their artful views. Plus there's a sit-down with a celebrated film director and, for good measure, an evening of karaoke with the J-pop cranked up high.

There's a lot to take in, including a first-rate line-up of the magazines and media houses that give readers a glimpse of the good life and offer advice on creating it for their readers. Read on and you'll soon see why Japan continues to catch the world's imagination.

Museums:
Art houses

Japan's museums consistently push the boundaries when it comes to displaying the country's cultural heritage. In these pages you'll encounter digital art, carpentry tools, ancient screens and a building that's both art installation and meditative space.

●

Mori Building Digital
Art Museum: TeamLab
Borderless
Tokyo

Imagine a museum where you can touch every artwork and where images are constantly changing and migrating from room to room, never exactly the same as when you first stood in front of them. All this is possible courtesy of TeamLab, a remarkable art collective that creates beautiful and immersive digital artworks and exhibits them to adoring crowds.

TeamLab was founded in 2001 by Toshiyuki Inoko, who – after finishing his studies in physics and mathematical engineering at Tokyo University – joined up with four friends to explore where maths, art and technology might meet. After designing websites and applications, work that is still a core part of the business, the opportunity to turn digital art into a viable business came in 2011 when Takashi Murakami – one of the biggest names in contemporary art – came across their work and offered them an exhibition space.

When Japanese developer Mori Building, which runs its own contemporary-art museum, heard that TeamLab wanted to build the first fully digital art museum, it rushed in. The firm offered to finance the project and provided a space in the Tokyo waterfront district of Odaiba. "We're using art and culture to make Tokyo a better place," says Ou Sugiyama from Mori Building, which runs operations at the museum.

There is growing interest in TeamLab's work from collectors. In 2014, Pace Gallery in New York started representing them and in 2018, "Ever Blossoming Life – Gold" sold at Christie's for $225,000 (€200,000). Inoko seems so focused on the work that he appears not to give too much thought to the mechanics of his company or the machinations of the art market. Yet he is a thinker. When he tries to explain why he creates art, he moves onto philosophy. The mission is complex and vast, from understanding the meaning of beauty to pulling people out of their smartphone-filtered worlds and into a shared public space that requires their physical presence.

You get the sense that it's almost too trying to explain – which is why Inoko has people like Takashi Kudo, another university friend and an eloquent advocate of TeamLab's aims. "We believe we can use digital art to change the relationship between humans and the world around them, as well as the relationship between people," he says. "In cities we can feel negative about people but here you can create and share a single moment of beauty with others that can't be repeated. It has the potential to make you feel more positive."

Brave new world
Nothing can quite prepare you for the discombobulating thrill of dipping into TeamLab's world. In one room at Borderless, "The Forest of Resonating Lamps", Venetian-glass lamps shine brighter when someone stands close, setting off a chain reaction with lights around them. Elsewhere, children watch in awe as their aquatic drawings are scanned and instantly float across the walls.

Takenaka Carpentry Museum
Kobe

For anyone who has ever wondered how Japan – a country with typhoons, extremely humid summers and bone-dry winters – manages to have some of the oldest wooden buildings in the world, the Takenaka Carpentry Tools Museum has the answers.

The museum, a beautiful repository of tools near Kobe's bullet train station, started as an ambitious project some 30 years ago. The then-chairman and president of construction giant Takenaka Corporation (which dates back to 1610) realised that the tools that had been so crucial to the development of the most sophisticated wood-building techniques in the world were in danger of disappearing. The company didn't have a collection and so every Takenaka branch office was put on alert and the great tool hunt began. Today the museum has 35,000 pieces in its collection, from *nokogiri* (saws) and *nomi* (chisels) to *kanna* (planes).

The museum, which opened in 1984, tells the history of building with wood in Japan and includes an array of tools and techniques, a teahouse and a life-size recreation of a 1,300-year-old interlocking pillar from a temple in Nara. The new museum building was designed to showcase Japanese *monozukuri* (craftsmanship): Yoshino cedar was used for the ceilings and frames, white oak for the floors and chestnut for the entrance door.

While the museum is largely a celebration of the past, it also hopes to inspire Japan's next generation of carpenters via a school outreach programme.

Art pavilion at Shinshoji Zen Museum and Gardens
Fukuyama

A wooden monolith that resembles a spaceship on stilts, the Kohtei art pavilion at Shinshoji Zen temple in Fukuyama city is the work of Japanese contemporary artist Kohei Nawa and his studio Sandwich. Completed in 2016, the building – which is set among a garden of stones and manicured shrubbery – incorporates traditional techniques: a master carpenter used bamboo nails to anchor 340,000 wooden shingles to create a gently curving *kokerabuki* (shingled roof).

Visitors enter the stone-floored chamber through a small opening that leads into darkness. As eyes adjust, the faint ripples of light on water become visible. Being inside the serene space is a spiritual experience of release akin to Zen meditation. Expressing spirituality through art has long been a feature of Zen Buddhism: the temple's gallery features a remarkable collection of paintings and calligraphy by Hakuin Ekaku, an influential monk who was active in the 18th century.

The art pavilion is one of several notable structures on the temple grounds, including a 17th-century hall, a recreation of a teahouse designed by tea master Sen no Rikyu and an office built from native pine trees by architect Terunobu Fujimori. The pavilion stands as a creative reinterpretation of the temple's teachings, a fusion of traditional and contemporary ideas and a sign of the ongoing evolution of Japanese Zen Buddhism.

Nezu Museum
Tokyo

This privately run museum in the centre of Tokyo first opened in 1941 in the former home of art collector and industrialist Kaichiro Nezu. In 2009 it reopened on the same site – a large Japanese garden dotted with traditional tea houses – in a discreet building designed by architect Kengo Kuma.

There are more than 7,000 pieces in its collection of Japanese and Chinese art, from sculpture and ceramics to paintings, textiles and calligraphy. Highlights include "Irises", a pair of screens painted by Korin Ogata in the 18th century, which are shown each spring to coincide with the flowering of the irises in the garden.

Archi-Depot
Tokyo has museums dedicated to everything from fireworks to socks but Archi-Depot is the first of its kind in Japan: an open archive of architectural models by some of Japan's best-known architects. It's both a storage and exhibition space, with 600 models kept at 20C and 50 per cent humidity. Guided tours of the curated selection on display are held six times a day.

Film:
Reel deal

Since producing its first silent films in the 19th century, Japan has built an idiosyncratic industry known for its originality and fresh approach: think anime, psycho-thrillers, Godzilla movies and samurai epics. So let's meet the country's premier director and sink into the seats of a few first-rate independent cinemas.

Cinema
Screen time

The popularity of internet streaming and high-definition television hasn't made it easy for the cinema industry. But lately cinema operators in Japan have been fighting back with an idea from the West: multiscreen complexes.

With more than 3,500 screens in Japan, the industry is in the midst of a comeback after decades of stagnation. Rising box-office sales have made Japanese cinemas more willing to take risks on films by unheralded directors and more likely to splurge on their facilities – think cafés, bars and concert hall-quality sound systems.

Japanese studios Toho, Shochiku, Toei and Kadokawa have responded by ramping up their output to roughly 600 films a year. Ranging from anime and *jidaigeki* (samurai period dramas) shot at Kyoto's Toei Studio Park to blockbuster action films, Japanese films now consistently outnumber western ones in cinemas – a reversal from the late 1980s when Hollywood imports ruled.

The resurgence has also created unexpected opportunities for independent theatres. Look no further than Uplink, a film distributor that runs two arthouse multi-screen cinemas in Tokyo and a third in a historic building in Kyoto. Its selection of the offbeat and obscure is a welcome antidote to celebrity-centric film-making.

For another view head to the seaside town of Zushi, southwest of Tokyo, where Gen Nagashima and Rai Shizuno run Cinema Amigo. With its eclectic collection of antique furniture, the venue is what cinemagoers would call a boutique experience but it's carved out a place for itself in the community.

Q&A
Hirokazu Koreeda

For more than a decade, Japanese film director Hirokazu Koreeda has put families at the centre of his work, challenging his country's ideas of love, death, poverty and kinship. Since *Shoplifters* won the Cannes Film Festival's Palme d'Or, he has had the chance to try new things. His 2019 film, *The Truth*, was his first overseas project involving actors who converse in French and English – two languages he doesn't speak.

Why are families the focus of your films?
I just make films about themes that I'm interested in. *Still Walking* was the first film I intentionally made about family. My mother had died and I had become a father. It was a time of big change in my life. Writing the screenplay helped me deal with my grief. Growing up, my family was like any other but with a slight disturbance on the surface. I like to draw out that: the small things that seem petty but matter.

Was 'Shoplifters', your film about a family of petty thieves who take in an abandoned child, meant to be critical of social norms in Japan?
I wrote the screenplay based on a news article but I didn't make the film to try to change the system. I never have, not even when I was making TV documentaries. I make films to explore a topic. They're a record of the process of my confronting my own prejudices and beliefs.

What made you take on 'The Truth'?
I've had a number of offers from overseas but it was Juliette Binoche who really persuaded me to make this film. Some French directors I know also encouraged me.

Japan on film

1.
Tokyo Story (1953)
Yasujiro Ozu
An understated family story in which traditionally minded parents visit their grown-up children in the big city only to be met with short shrift and modern manners. It's a masterpiece that defines Japan's celluloid register: subtle, memorable, devastating.

2.
Seven Samurai (1954)
Akira Kurosawa
Kurosawa's bandit-busting epic was remade many times – as westerns, in space, even with animated insects – but only after the great director himself had seen and admired John Ford and the Hollywood method.

3.
Nobody Knows (2004)
Hirokazu Koreeda
A mother leaves her children to run wild in a Tokyo apartment while she pursues a romance. Koreeda's style tips between fiction and documentary as the children's strange world unfolds in this perfect exercise in heartstrings teased, not tugged.

4.
My Neighbour Totoro (1988)
Hayao Miyazaki
Two sisters befriend Nature – in the form of Totoro, a woodland sprite – when they spend a summer in the country. Miyazaki's animated universe sits somewhere between Lewis Carroll and Godzilla. Whimsy with a spine of steel.

5.
Your Name (2016)
Makoto Shinkai
A boy-girl, city-country body-swap romance may sound a super hokey confection but Shinkai's universe is one of significance, subtlety and a knowledge that actions reap consequences.

Comment: *The world of Hayao Miyazaki — Mark Schilling, film critic*

In the early 1990s the Japanese film industry was at rock bottom in both production numbers and box-office returns. Out of this darkness arose a new generation of film-makers who owed little or nothing to the studio system of the past and instead made low-budget films in lightly regarded genres.

In 1997, animation maestro Hayao Miyazaki released *Princess Mononoke*, a fantasy set in medieval Japan that became the highest-earning Japanese film of all time. Its record was beaten four years later by *Spirited Away*, Miyazaki's tale of a girl who slips into a world of gods and spirits. Released in 2001, it signalled the start of a new era in which Japanese films – both animated and live-action – would dominate their Hollywood rivals.

Since then, the Japanese film-makers who were prominent internationally at the turn of the millennium have continued to receive the lion's share of overseas critical attention. In the anime world there has been more ferment with putative successors to Miyazaki emerging in a steady stream, while the most popular Japanese live-action films abroad have continued to tilt to the cult end of the scale.

Media:
Press ahead

Japan is a nation of devoted newspaper readers. For the most part, its traditional media giants have held their own in the face of an onslaught from online upstarts. We take a look at the leading papers and magazines that are setting the agenda and drop in on a popular online messaging service.

The Nikkei
When it comes to business news in Japan, *The Nikkei* – the biggest financial newspaper in the world – has few rivals. Even with strict rules on how and when listed companies communicate with investors, the national daily is often the first to bring pertinent information to its nearly 3 million print and online readers. The paper's €1.2bn acquisition of the *Financial Times* in 2015 put ownership of one of the world's top business newspapers into the hands of a company with clout in Japan but little name recognition globally. *The Nikkei* is also a Monocle investor.

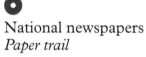

National newspapers
Paper trail

Japan sells 46 million papers a day, a staggering figure in a country of just under 127 million, and its 116 daily newspapers compete for attention in a crowded field. At the top of the pile are five national dailies led by the *Yomiuri Shimbun*, founded in 1874. Delivering nearly 8 million copies nationwide each day, and offering both morning and evening print editions, it ranks as the world's best-selling newspaper.

As is the case at many companies in Japan, the paper's journalists have little say when it comes to choosing their assignments – someone who is a crime reporter one day might be transferred to public relations, for example – and they almost never become household names. With the exception of the infrequent investigative features and some dispatches from overseas bureaux, bylines are extremely rare.

The *Yomiuri* has access to the highest echelons of powers and its right-of-centre editorials tend to align with the ruling Liberal Democratic party – something that has fuelled allegations that the paper shies away from hard-hitting stories about influential figures. It's a different story for the paper's biggest rival, the *Asahi Shimbun*, founded in 1879. The second-largest of the national dailies, this centre-left paper uses its access to frequently target what its editors see as misguided public policies – one reason for its often-testy relations with senior government officials.

For all of the national dailies, the days of sky-high circulation may be numbered: even with the papers' efforts to sell digital subscriptions, the rise of online media sites continues to erode their empires.

Tabloids
The mainstream national dailies are hardly the best at scoring scoops. For that, you're better off scanning the pages of daily *supotsu shimbun* (sports newspaper) tabloids and news weeklies *Shukan Bunshun*, *Shukan Shincho*, *Shukan Gendai* and *Shukan Post*. That's where you'll find stories about murders, suicides, the sex trade, organised crime and politicians' affairs. Without the connections to power, these papers aren't concerned about upsetting authorities and publishing stories with salacious details.

Line
Tokyo

Online messaging service Line is a household name in Japan and across Asia. The Tokyo-based company (owned by South Korean technology firm Naver) launched its smartphone app in 2011, three months after a massive earthquake and tsunami hit Japan's northeastern seaboard. The disaster had disrupted lives, businesses and communications, and the free messaging app created a means of reaching loved ones when phone lines were down.

But what truly set Line apart would come a few months later: virtual "stickers" featuring cartoon characters that users could send in lieu of texts. Today, some 82 million people at home and 82 million abroad use Line. Two million businesses have signed up to create stickers for users to choose from.

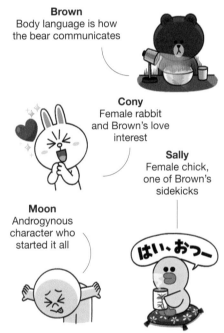

Brown
Body language is how the bear communicates

Cony
Female rabbit and Brown's love interest

Sally
Female chick, one of Brown's sidekicks

Moon
Androgynous character who started it all

Magazine House
Tokyo

Lifestyle and fashion publisher Magazine House occupies unobtrusive digs on a slender back street in Higashi Ginza, a few steps behind Tokyo's most famous kabuki theatre. Inside are the editorial homes of magazines that many Japanese have grown up with, including *Popeye*, the fashion magazine "for city boys", *Brutus*, the thinking man's fortnightly and *Ginza*, a women's magazine with an eye beyond the world of frocks.

Founded by Kinosuke Iwahori and Tatsuo Shimizu in October 1945, this publishing grandaddy has helped guide Japan's cultural conversation. These may be testing times but Magazine House's titles are lapped up by readers in bookshops all over Asia.

1

2

3

4

5

6

7

Magazines:
Page turners

Japan is a paradise for print lovers, with more than 2,700 magazine titles serving every age group and niche interest. Here we leaf through journals covering a range of topics, from design and dog breeding to casual fashion.

8   9

10   11

1.
Pen
A twice-a-month men's culture and lifestyle journal.

2.
Popeye
This fashion-and-culture monthly is aimed at young men.

3.
Hail Mary
A men's monthly on casual US fashion and culture.

4.
Mark
A running and sports-culture biannual.

5.
Sumu
Sumu means "to live" and its main focus is the home: from architecture and children's furniture to gardens and recipes. Launched in 2002, the magazine is a better-living how-to and works on many levels, showcasing cosy residences and chronicling how the owners built them.

6.
Yama to Keikoku
This monthly magazine focuses on mountaineering and trekking.

7.
Ginza
A women's high-fashion and urban-culture monthly.

8.
Onkul
A biannual journal of fashion basics for young women.

9.
Men's Club
Monthly musings for men interested in style, fashion and beauty.

10.
&Premium
A culture-and-lifestyle monthly for women.

11.
Go Out
This monthly magazine is about all things outdoor fashion and style.

12–13.
Brutus and Casa Brutus
If lifestyle magazine *Brutus* is what fans of design, fashion and dining (with a dose of films, books and music) turn to for their fix, then its sister monthly, *Casa Brutus*, is the equivalent for anyone who loves interior design and architecture.

14
Sports Graphic Number
Reading material for athletes and the sporting world, published twice a month.

7

12   13

15.
Idea
Japan's graphic-art and typography quarterly got its start in 1953 and helped to elevate graphic design as a profession in the country's corporate world. *Idea*'s editorial team showcases posters, advertisements and signs but also leaves plenty of room for extensive coverage of the best in the US and Europe.

16.
Wan
This dog lovers' journal is published every other month.

17.
Switch
Monthly interviews with creatives and entertainers.

18.
Shukan Shincho
A hard-hitting news weekly.

19.
Shukyu
A biannual on football culture and fashion.

20.
Hobby Journal
All you need to know about plastic model kits.

21.
Mamor
This monthly journal covers all things defence and military.

22.
Dancyu
There are many ways to cook a salmon and *Dancyu* will happily devote an issue to showing you more techniques than you'll ever use (plus how to flavour the roe) while also exploring how the fish gets to your table. Founded in 1990, the magazine's deep dives into cooking, speciality restaurants and hidden bars are for the weekend chef and the food-obsessed.

23.
Weekly Shonen Jump
A weekly serialised manga for boys.

24.
Tsuru & Hana
If you're after tips for ageing gracefully.

25.
Hanako
A food-and-travel monthly for young women.

26.
Kunel
Fashion, beauty and food for women 50 and up. After a revamp in 2016, the magazine shifted to focus on chic older women.

27.
Spectator
A triannual journal on alternative subcultures.

28.
Turns
A collection of stories from across Japan, published every other month.

14   15

16 17

20 21

18 19

22

23

24 25

27

26   28

Books:
Novel ideas

Print has never been so in demand, especially at Daikanyama T-site's Tsutaya Books in Tokyo. It's a model for success in a country where publishing houses release more than 75,000 new book titles a year. We browse through this bountiful bookshop and others, and catch up on some Japanese best sellers.

Bunkitsu
Tokyo

Bunkitsu is first and foremost a bookshop, albeit a ticketed one. It may seem elitist but the company behind it – Nippon Shuppan Hanbai (Nippan), one of Japan's biggest book distributors – believes its approach will reawaken an appreciation for literature. The ¥1,500 (€12) entry fee isn't for nothing. There is a café and the rest of the space encourages people to linger without feeling rushed to make a purchase. A quiet reading zone and research room are accessible past the admission-fee barrier while magazines are free to browse.

Musashino Place library
Musashino

Designed by KW + HG Architects in Tokyo, this library and community centre in Musashino has more than 180,000 books, 600 periodical titles and 400 seats that anyone with a card can use. The city wanted it to be open to all ages, with the emphasis on lifelong learning. Teens have their own space for dance, craft and music classes while younger children have a reading area and a room for story-time. With this warm, curvy building, the architects have shown that municipal design can be both functional and inviting.

Daikanyama Tsutaya Books
Tokyo

In an ever-changing landscape of big-box media retailers, it's not easy to come by a formula for success. But when Muneaki Masuda, founder and president of Culture Convenience Club (CCC), opened Daikanyama Tsutaya Books in Tokyo in late 2011, it was an instant hit.

Designed by Tokyo-based Klein Dytham Architecture, the bookshop stretches across three two-storey buildings and features 140,000 books, 30,000 magazines, 100,000 CDs and 100,000 DVDs. But it's the extras that elevate the shopping experience. In the travel area is a desk where travel agents can arrange flights or hotels, and the stationery section has hundreds of pens to choose from. For children, there are DVDs and picture books. And the central Anjin lounge and bar, with its vintage magazines and a grand piano ready for live performances, is ideal for unwinding with a glass of wine.

The complex is easy to navigate thanks to signs by graphic designer Kenya Hara and plenty of iPads. A true cultural hub, it's brimming with customers until closing at 02.00. In fact, the concept has proven so popular that CCC has since opened 23 more Tsutaya Books and been commissioned to revamp several public libraries.

Japan in print
Since Murasaki Shikibu's 11th-century masterpiece *The Tale of Genji*, Japanese literature has flourished and evolved. Here are five from the modern literary canon.

**1.
Kokoro (1914)**
Natsume Soseki
This work by one of Japan's greatest novelists centres on a young man's friendship with an older man who shares a story of guilt about his past.

**2.
Snow Country (1937)**
Yasunari Kawabata
A classic of Japanese literature, this book is set in the mountains of Niigata and chronicles a local geisha's doomed love affair with a wealthy visitor from Tokyo. Kawabata was Japan's first winner of the Nobel Prize in Literature.

**3.
The Makioka Sisters (1943-1948)**
Junichiro Tanizaki
The most acclaimed of Tanizaki's novels follows four sisters living in Osaka in the 1930s. The sisters' contrasting views about marriage and society mirror the tensions of a modernising society.

**4.
Norwegian Wood (1987)**
Haruki Murakami
The novel that elevated Murakami to worldwide literary stardom dwells on the unresolved grief of a man who remembers his love for a troubled woman who committed suicide.

**5.
Convenience Store Woman (2016)**
Sayaka Murata
The first of Murata's best-sellers to be translated, this story about a woman who works at a convenience store is a critique of a conformist society that expects people to fill predestined roles.

Manga
Visit the manga section of any bookshop in Japan and prepare to be overwhelmed. From children's comics to graphic novels with intricate storylines, manga has mainstream appeal. Manga titles are bestsellers too: the manga version of *Kimitachi Wa Do Ikiru Ka* (*How Do You Live?*), originally written by Genzaburo Yoshino in 1937, topped the book industry's sales ranking for 2018.

With its roots in woodblock prints and illustrated scrolls, this storytelling art form has gained in popularity since the Second World War and influenced sectors from fashion and art to video games. The biggest titles – Osamu Tezuka's *Tetsuwan Atomu* (*Astro Boy*), Fujiko F Fujio's *Doraemon* and Eiichiro Oda's *One Piece* series, to name a few – have become blockbuster film franchises and many top musicians, artists and athletes have cited manga as the inspiration for their careers.

Annual revenues from the manga business top ¥441bn (€3.6bn) – nearly half from online and e-book sales – and the appeal of Japanese cultural exports offers the potential for reaching new audiences.

Theatre:
Playing a part

Japan's traditional performing arts are laced with extravagant flourishes and dramatic plot twists. The spectacle is a must, especially as performers are exploring new ways to bring their craft to a younger audience.

Theatre
Set the stage

It's not always easy to follow the plot twists in a *kabuki* performance. But the betrayals, shifting alliances and mistaken identities are part of the entertaining spectacle of this traditional form of Japanese theatre. With roots that go back to the 17th century, *kabuki* is performed by an all-male cast of face-painted actors, featuring stories that unfold to singing and music. For the biggest stars – some known as *onnagata*, men who specialise in playing female roles – it's a profession and an inheritance: they learn from their fathers and grandfathers and teach their own children and grandchildren in turn.

Like many of Japan's ancient dramatic arts, *kabuki* is caught between its own weighty traditions and modern society. Practitioners of *noh* (dance-drama), *bunraku* (puppetry), *buyo* (traditional dance) and *gagaku* (court music) face a similar challenge. Even as they train to master intricate movements and songs that have been passed down for generations, they must be willing to break with orthodoxy to stay relevant while also stepping into their roles as cultural ambassadors, performing for audiences overseas and reaching out to young people.

Music:
Tune in

J-pop may rule the airwaves and streaming playlists but there are many more dimensions to Japanese popular music, from film and animation soundtracks to traditional ballads and age-old folk songs.

J-pop
Band together

J-pop is Japanese pop music. It's boy bands and girl groups, rappers and soloists, rock bands and teenage heavy-metal acts. It's earnest and sentimental and it's big business: CDs, downloads, streaming data, videos and karaoke playlists. The catchall term was first used in the 1990s to market it to an international audience. The irony is that, while big at home, most of these groups still barely register on the global stage.

Boy bands have long ruled J-pop and talent agency Johnny & Associates has been behind the biggest chart-toppers: Smap beginning in the late 1980s, Arashi in the late 1990s and 2000s and King & Prince more recently. They dance and sing in sync, merging hummable mid-tempo pop and Broadway dance steps. They sell millions of records, fill arenas and for a while they're everywhere, from TV to billboard advertisements.

They compete for attention with the girl group AKB48, a 107-member project with spinoffs and sister acts. A few female musicians with signature looks have tried their luck overseas but their limited global appeal has exposed how much Japanese celebrities depend on the media's sympathetic treatment.

Beyond those groups, there's plenty of diversity, from R&B singer Hikaru Utada to guitar band Bump of Chicken. The new generation of mainstream stars – singer-songwriter Aimyon and rock band Official Hige Dandism – is winning over young fans with a genre-blurring version of pop that's experimenting with technology and stretching the category even further.

Vinyl shops
Go for a spin

Tiny record stores abound in Japan and their very existence points to a thriving subculture that's helping to introduce a new generation to the joys of this old-fashioned audio technology.

Waltz, *Tokyo*
Cassette tapes, boomboxes and vinyl records can be found in abundance at this neighbourhood music shop in Nakameguro. Swimming against the tide of digital technology, Waltz focuses on the unique qualities of analog media. More than just a trip down memory lane, it also carries a range of new releases and reissues.

Ella Records, *Tokyo*
In the cute neighbourhood of Nishihara, Shigeki Kuzuhara's diminutive record shop is perfect for anyone who wants to get into vinyl. On offer is a tight selection of 3,500 records that covers everything from classics to rarities, with a particularly strong selection of Japanese music. This is the place to get deeper into Japanese Jazz, Folk and New Wave and become better acquainted with the likes of Yellow Magic Orchestra and Tatsuro Yamashita.

Especial Records, *Osaka*
Yoshihiro Okino was a young DJ working in Osaka's underground club scene when he opened Especial Records in 1998. He started off selling records that he'd bought during trips to London and jazz crossover, soul and Brazilian are still genres that he favours. Okino now sits behind the shop's counter while also working on music for his label – including his own group, Kyoto Jazz Massive, which he heads with his older brother Shuya.

Festivals
Japan's calendar is crammed with music festivals – more than 100 during the peak period in summer. Fuji Rock at Naeba Ski Resort in Niigata and Summer Sonic, a weekend event in Tokyo and Osaka, draw the industry's big names – a mix of rock headliners and pop, indie and punk bands – and as many as 300,000 people.

Other music events around the country and throughout the year cater to reggae, world music and J-pop fans. Outdoor venues include Rock in Japan in Ibaraki, Rising Sun Rock Festival in Hokkaido and Sunset Live in Fukuoka, while Countdown Japan – held in late December in Chiba – has the final acts of the year.

If a community-led event is a better fit, opt for Good Neighbors Jamboree, an open-air craft fair, garden party and music festival at an abandoned primary school in Kagoshima.

155

Karaoke:
Hitting the high notes

Japan's karaoke salons are all about disco lights, cigarette-scented rooms, plenty of drinks and slurred vocals. It's a much-loved shared experience and is more about giving it a go with gusto than perfect pitch.

●

Bonenkai Season
Sing a song

There's something about the end-of-year holiday spirit and a few rounds of drinks that can bring out the crooner in just about anyone in Japan. For office workers and old friends across the country, December is peak season for *bonenkai* – parties to forget the year – and no gathering would be complete without karaoke.

It's easy to imagine the post-dinner setting: a dimly lit private room with a padded U-shaped bench, microphones, wireless tablets for selecting songs and a large flat-screen TV. There are tambourines and maracas, fried dishes, towering glasses of shochu highballs and mugs of beer; sometimes there are even costumes.

Daisuke Inoue invented the karaoke machine in 1971, turning public singing into a beloved national pastime. While it's usually performed at a bar on a stage in front of a roomful of people in the West, the Japanese prefer the privacy of a small room – and there are no shortage of places to belt out a few tunes. Today there are more than 130,000 rooms at 9,265 karaoke salons and bars around the country.

Though the popularity peaked in the mid-1990s, with 58.9 million devotees, there's no sign that Japan's karaoke fever is dying. In fact, it's become such a fixture at end-of-the-year parties that some people even rent a booth alone for a couple of hours of practice beforehand. It makes sense: the *bonenkai* is the perfect chance to trot out your singing skills, impress your colleagues and win points with your boss – not to mention having the chance to feel like a pop star.

156

Top karaoke tunes

1.
Christmas Eve
Tatsuro Yamashita
One of the elder statesmen of Japanese pop, Yamashita released "Christmas Eve" on his 1983 album *Melodies* but the song didn't immediately hit the charts. It took a railway company's TV commercial to solidify its status as a Christmas standard.

2.
Choo Choo Train
Exile
Boy band Exile's hit from the early 2000s pays homage to disco and R&B. The lyrics of this infectiously danceable number switch between English and Japanese in a jumble that's hard to comprehend and a joy to sing.

3.
Ue Wo Muite Aruko
Kyu Sakamoto
The lilting melody of this tune from the early 1960s masks the message in the lyrics, which reveal Sakamoto's frustration after a student demonstration to protest against the US military occupation after the end of the Second World War.

4.
Machigai Sagashi
Masaki Suda
A promising young actor, Suda launched his solo music career in 2017 and released this song – "Looking for Mistakes" – about personal struggle in 2019.

5.
Itoshi no Erii (Ellie My Love)
Southern All Stars
This pop ballad from 1979 is a classic of Southern All Stars' songbook. Ray Charles performed a cover of the song in English for a Japanese TV commercial in the late 1980s and added it to his *Would You Believe?* album in 1990.

Comment: *In praise of singing — Tyler Brûlé*

Karaoke and MONOCLE go a long way back – all the way to the launch of the magazine in 2007 when the founding team spent a very long night high above Roppongi belting out tunes, donning wigs and clanging along with tambourines. Since then our tastes have become more refined, voices have improved and we've found our 'spots' in neighbourhoods across Japan – Ginza and Shinjuku Ni-chome are favourite haunts.

While rumours have circulated that a position in our Tokyo bureau demands a proper audition (or at the very least a singing sample should accompany the CV) we can confirm that this is not the case as two of our most senior colleagues never go anywhere near the mic, though they don't mind shaking a maraca now and then.

As cultural exports go, we feel that Japan deserves considerably more credit for refining a concept that has helped soften corporate hierarchies, bolster night-time economies, spawn countless TV formats, launch a thousand pop careers and remind us that everyone can find their range and sing along with The Carpenters.

157

3

三

Design and architecture

デザインと建築

Few countries have influenced the course of global architecture and design more meaningfully than Japan. The nation's Shinto shrines and ancient temples rightly draw crowds but there's also a constellation of more contemporary buildings to consider.

In this chapter we profile 10 seminal structures, from the sleek and sparkling to the boxy, bulky and at times bizarre. In Japan, buildings are routinely scrapped and rebuilt at a frightening pace, which helps to showcase the versatility of the talent here.

In terms of graphic design, you needn't look much further than the country's simple but superb flag to see how the subtle grace of good branding can elevate people's estimations of a place – and other examples abound. In industrial design too, Japan's successes are tied up with a long history of honouring craft that means whole villages and even regions specialise in products such as bentwood bento boxes and cast-iron cookware.

From tatami mats and towering new-builds to Toto toilets, Japan is – ahem – flush with inspiring and design-minded solutions.

Ten buildings:
Striking structures

Architecture is one of Japan's most valuable soft-power assets. Here we take a tour of both traditional and contemporary creations by some of the country's top talents.

1.
Sumida Hokusai
Museum
Kazuyo Sejima, 2016

Katsushika Hokusai's woodblock print of a towering wave with Mount Fuji in the background is one of the most iconic images in Japanese art. Hokusai was born in the Sumida district of Tokyo in 1760 and lived to be nearly 90. In 2016 the city finally opened a museum dedicated to one of its most famous sons.

Designed by Pritzker Prize-winning architect Kazuyo Sejima (one half of architecture studio SANAA), the museum sits in a park that is close to Hokusai's birthplace. Taking care of the artist's work within is key, which means carefully controlling light levels: the outside walls are made from aluminium panels but slits in the exterior are glazed so daylight is allowed to filter in.

2.

Teshima Art Museum
Ryue Nishizawa, 2010

Tadao Ando may be the first name that springs to mind when it comes to Japanese concrete architecture but Ryue Nishizawa's Teshima Art Museum gives Ando a run for his money. Completed in 2010 on an island in the Seto Inland Sea, the structure was tailor-made to house a single piece of work by the artist Rei Naito. The museum is the perfect showpiece for the outstanding engineering of Japanese construction giant Kajima Corporation. It took an army of skilled workers 26 hours to cast the concrete in one enormous, seamless shell, which covers the roughly 2,300 sq m space without the use of pillars or other supports. Nishizawa (one half of architecture studio SANAA) incorporated two large holes in the 25cm-thick dome, connecting the people inside with the nature outside.

Island design
Benesse Holdings and the Fukutake Foundation have transformed the islands of Naoshima, Teshima and Inujima by commissioning top architects to build exhibition spaces.

3.
**Kogakuin University
Archery Hall**
FT Architects, 2013

Tokyo-based FT Architects designed this tucked-away archery hall for Kogakuin University in 2013. To keep costs down, the studio used discarded timber, and created a design that riffs on the vertical and horizontal combinations of pillars and beams frequently found in Japan's traditional wooden buildings.

The result is a delicate lattice framework (a nod to the forms and dynamism of the bow and arrow) that not only serves a functional purpose but also adds character to the space. With the help of experts, simple wooden pieces were developed that could be screwed together on-site. A great example of how tradition can be kept alive and relevant.

Aim high
Sport has inspired some impressive Japanese architecture including Kenzo Tange's Yoyogi National Gymnasium and the Nippon Budokan martial arts hall by Mamoru Yamada.

4.
Katsura Rikyu
17th century

Following the lead of German architect Bruno Taut, a generation of European modernists discovered the exquisite simplicity of Katsura Rikyu in the early 20th century and the love affair continues today. The stripped-back beauty of this 17th-century Imperial villa and garden in western Kyoto surprises with its minimalism, geometry and apparent modernity.

The buildings are almost entirely bereft of ornamentation and constructed from little more than wood and paper – even the shelves and door handles are celebrated and studied for their abstract forms. There are three palace buildings, four teahouses, a moon-viewing veranda and a network of bridges and stone lanterns scattered throughout the landscaped grounds.

5.
Kyoto International Conference Centre
Sachio Otani, 1966

For sheer eccentricity, it's hard to beat Kyoto's International Conference Centre (ICC). Designed by Sachio Otani and completed in 1966, it's a prime example of Metabolism, an architectural movement that briefly flourished in postwar Japan and was led by architects Fumihiko Maki, Kiyonori Kikutake and Kisho Kurokawa.

The movement examined the future of urban architecture as the economy boomed and cities were expanding at high speed. Metabolism was often more of a concept than a reality but it was rich in ideas, especially at the 1970 Expo in Osaka.

The ICC is one of the few built examples, a concrete structure that references Japan's traditional shrines and A-frame wooden houses while looking unlike anything else that had come before. One highlight is the interior design created by modernist Isamu Kenmochi, who was inspired by the shapes and materials of traditional Japanese craft.

Kenzo Tange's Shizuoka Press and Broadcasting Centre in Tokyo (1967) is another example, and perhaps the best known is Kurokawa's Nakagin Capsule Tower from 1972, which envisaged the future apartment building as a stack of pre-fab pods. Although it was never replicated as planned, the original tower still stands in Tokyo, somewhat dishevelled.

6.
Church of the Light
Tadao Ando, 1989

Boxer-turned-architect Tadao Ando has done more than any other to create the perception of contemporary Japan as a world of concrete minimalism. Famously self-taught, Ando has repeatedly shown the poetic potential of concrete in works such as Church of the Light, which he built in 1989 in Ibaraki, a city just outside Osaka.

This small Christian chapel is a work of beauty that draws architecture pilgrims from around the world. Although Ando is never one to look back, the church has come to be seen as a defining work and was even recreated for a Tokyo retrospective of the architect's oeuvre.

7.
The National Art
Centre Tokyo
Kisho Kurokawa, 2006

Among Kisho Kurokawa's final works, this vast art centre in the Roppongi neighbourhood of Tokyo includes 12 galleries, a restaurant, three cafés, a shop and an art library. There is no permanent collection but the building hosts a roster of temporary art shows and offers a space in which visitors can sit or stroll.

The undulating façade – a wave created from thousands of glass panels – made the art centre an instant landmark. The structure is also notable for its technical aspects: seismic isolation devices absorb the judder from earthquakes while features such as rainwater reuse and underfloor air conditioning save energy. Kurokawa's work was never less than challenging but this building was deemed one of his most successful.

8.
Toukouen Hotel
Kiyonori Kikutake, 1964

Perched at the westernmost edge of Tottori, Japan's least populous prefecture, the city of Yonago has long drawn visitors to its beachfront hotels. Among these is Toukouen, an old establishment which was partially (and dramatically) rebuilt in the 1960s by Kiyonori Kikutake.

Kikutake created a remarkable work of modernism that remains largely unbothered by renovation today. Buffeted by harsh Japan Sea winds, the hotel offers a remote retreat and terrific views of the sea and volcanic Mount Daisen. The therapeutic, salty hot-spring water is piped into a bath house, which was designed by sculptor Masayuki Nagare, who also added the Japanese garden. Emperor Hirohito came to visit the building in 1965 and Kikutake added another wing a few years later.

Modernist masters
Key names in Japanese modernism include Kunio Maekawa, Junzo Yoshimura and Junzo Sakakura, who worked with Le Corbusier in Paris.

9.
Kagawa Prefectural
Office East Building
Kenzo Tange, 1958

Like so much of Japanese modernism, Kenzo Tange's Kagawa Prefectural Office in the city of Takamatsu harks back to traditional architecture. Built in 1958, it was a collaboration between Tange (one of Japan's finest postwar architects), visionary furniture designer Isamu Kenmochi and artist Genichiro Inokuma, who created a mural for the ground-floor lobby called *"Wakeiseijaku"* (Harmony, Respect, Purity, Tranquility).

Former governor Masanori Kaneko hoped the building would convey a sense of democracy; the rooftop, which has views over the Seto Inland Sea, was open to the public. Tange went on to have a stellar career, creating several works around Setouchi and the Yoyogi National Gymnasium for the 1964 Tokyo Olympics.

10.
Ise Shrine
Anonymous

Japan is famous for its unsentimental attitude towards old buildings and renewal is also deeply ingrained in the culture. No stranger to fires, wars and natural disasters, the nation has rebuilt myriad structures and even some entire cities. When it comes to traditional architecture, Ise

Jingu in Mie prefecture, the most important Shinto shrine in Japan, holds the key to understanding many aspects of the Japanese approach.

Ise's history stretches back 2,000 years and the site exercises a tradition called *shikinen sengu*, which involves demolishing and rebuilding some of the key ancient Japanese structures – built with solid hinoki cypress wood – every 20 years. First conducted in 690, the practice is crucial to keeping the know-how and skills alive.

Making a mark
The wooden structures of Shinto shrines and Buddhist temples are built by highly skilled carpenters called *miyadaiku*. They have the expertise to puzzle timbers together without nails and the knowledge to create structures that survive for centuries. Their history dates back to the seventh century.

Residences:
House and home

There are lessons to be learned from Japan's cosy and livable homes, which are designed at just the right scale and arc always in harmony with their environment – whether that's urban or natural. Of the countless doors we've knocked on over the years, here are our highlights.

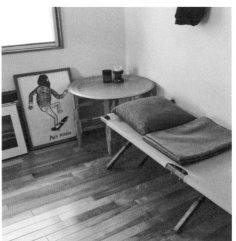

Residence 1
Nasu

When it comes to design, the Japanese and Scandinavians share a penchant for warm, natural materials and utility over embellishment. As such, spotting a handsome Swedish-style timber lodge in the middle of a Japanese mountain range happens more frequently than you might imagine.

Shoichiro Aiba, the owner and chef of popular Tokyo restaurant Life, fell for such a cabin when visiting leafy Hokkaido on a catering job. Its design came courtesy of Sweden House, a Japanese company that's built a cult

following for its quick-to-install, cool-in-summer, warm-in-winter timber homes made from Scandinavian materials.

After researching the brand, Aiba purchased a secondhand Sweden House of his own in Nasu, a mountainous region with clear streams and hot springs just a three-hour drive from Tokyo. The property is surrounded by trees and receives lots of natural light filtering through the foliage and its big square windows.

"We're not hardcore outdoor people so it's good to have a place like this to get out to," says Aiba of his family's second home. "It's not too close or too far. It gives you the sense that you are travelling."

170

● Residence 2
Tokyo

In Japan's densely populated cities, space is at a premium – and nowhere more so than in Tokyo. When architect Takeshi Hosaka bought a tiny parcel of land in the city, his challenge was to build a smart and comfortable home in a plot not much bigger than a parking space. The 19 sq m concrete house he designed and now lives in is a prime example of quality living on a small scale.

"My wife pointed out that in the Edo period a family of four would live in a home that covers four and a half tatami mats," says Takeshi. "We're two people so, actually, this is not small," says his wife, Megumi.

Like an astronomer, Takeshi calculated the orbit of the sun to design the shape of the roof. He cut a skylight in the seven-metre-high ceiling so they could receive maximum sunlight without having to stare at the apartment block behind.

"Ancient Romans valued five things: bath, music, food, theatre and books – and so do we," says Takeshi. The home accommodates hundreds of books and records, a practical kitchen, a queen-size bed and an outdoor bath. Admiring architects have visited and the duo's friends regularly come for dinner parties. "We're not minimalists," adds Takeshi. "We didn't give up anything."

It's one of the ironies of Japan's economic superpower status that the average Japanese family's home is a fraction of the size of homes in less wealthy nations, forcing them to become specialists in space-saving know-how. Appliance shops stock slimline toasters and coffee pots that don't take up much counter space, while department stores sell cotton futon mattresses that are pulled out and slept on at night and folded away during the day.

173

Residence 3
Asahikawa

The small Hokkaido city of Asahikawa is best known for its concentration of wooden-furniture makers. It's fitting then that it's here you'll find the home of Noritsugu Oda, owner of one of the world's most impressive collections of chairs (1,350 at the last count, more than half of them Danish).

Surrounded by birch trees that he planted himself, the house is filled with the chairs, lights, pottery and glass that Oda has acquired over the years. Every drawer is crammed with cutlery and pens while dozens of Iittala glass birds are scattered about. But this is no museum: everything in the house is comfortable and well-used, from the Bruno Mathsson reclining chair to the Poul Kjærholm circular dining table.

Nor is Oda a Scandinavian purist; you'll find Japanese dolls from his father, who worked for the Imperial Household Agency, cosying up to a Korean kettle and a mask from Burkina Faso. "Danish design is very functional," he says, pointing to a rare Danish sideboard made in the 1930s. "The makers thought about how people would use the furniture, even down to the size of the plates. You never tire of it."

Design icons:
Form and function

Japanese design is both elegant and enduring. We've crisscrossed the nation to pick out some prime examples that represent its pursuit of quality, attention to detail and sheer beauty.

1964 Olympics poster
Japan's proficiency in graphic design shows in its logos and packaging. The 1964 Tokyo Olympics was a high point, with memorable posters and the first use of sporting pictograms.

Olympus Pen EE-2
Half-frame cameras were a trend in Japan in the 1960s, offering twice the number of frames on a regular roll of film. The original Olympus Pen was designed by Yoshihisa Maitani in 1959 while this Pen EE-2 appeared in 1968.

Paper lantern
The *chochin* (paper lantern) comes in many forms; at its simplest it's made of *washi* (paper) pasted onto a bamboo frame and gives a welcoming glow. Japanese-American sculptor Isamu Noguchi designed his own versions which are still made in Gifu today.

Honda Super Cub
A sturdy workhorse, the Honda Super Cub – in production since 1958 – is a ubiquitous sight on city streets, used for delivering post, newspapers and noodles.

Sensu fan
A light, slim, folding *sensu* (fan) – made of wood and *washi* – is the simplest solution for the humid Japanese summer. Its history goes back to Kyoto in the ninth century.

Butterfly stool
Beloved designer Sori Yanagi's moulded plywood Butterfly stool for Japanese wooden furniture company Tendo Mokko is a classic from 1954.

Zen garden
The *karesansui* (dry landscape) often known as a Zen garden creates a world in abstracted miniature where rocks, stones and a few plants symbolise nature on a grand scale.

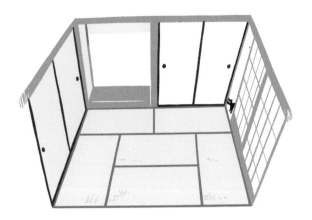

Tatami mat
The tatami mat is both an object and a measure of room size. The fresh smell of *igusa* (soft rush) and the light green colour (which gradually turns golden) set a uniquely Japanese tone. There are hundreds of patterns for the belt running along the edge of the mat.

Toto toilet
Wash and blow-dry toilets are a standard feature in Japanese homes. Toto leads the way and the Neorest model combines state-of-the-art technology with a simple silhouette.

Tei zaisu
As Japan transitioned from traditional wooden homes, hybrid pieces like the *tei zaisu* (low chair) by Daisaku Choh emerged. Released in 1960, it works well on tatami mats or wooden floors.

Randoseru
All primary school children in Japan carry these leather rucksacks known as *randoseru* (borrowed from the old Dutch word *ransel*). Often a hefty investment for parents, the boxy bags have to last for six years.

Tea whisk
The *chasen* (bamboo whisk) is an essential part of the *chanoyu* (tea ceremony). Used to whip matcha green tea into a rich froth, it's carved from a single piece of bamboo.

Muji hut
Like Sori Yanagi before him, product designer Naoto Fukasawa keeps things simple, sticking firmly to the concept of function over frivolous details. His work for Muji includes this timber hut, a wooden prefab that can be built anywhere.

Pruning scissors
A Japanese gardener is likely to wear *jika-tabi* (split-toed shoes) and a *tenugui* headscarf; among the essential tools in the leather belt will be these gardening scissors.

Soy-sauce dispenser
Designed in 1958 by Masahiro Mori, this soy-sauce dispenser is a long-standing bestseller, which is made in the ceramic village of Hasami by Hakusan Porcelain.

Craft:
Handmade tale

Japan may be forward-thinking but it's also immensely proud of its heritage. These age-old crafts continue to be handed down from generation to generation.

1.
Woodwork
Natural resource

Japan's forested mountainous terrain has made wood the primary building material for everything from houses to temples for centuries. The town of Odate in Akita has become synonymous with one particular wooden craft – *magewappa* (bentwood) – and the chosen material is Akita *sugi*, a majestic native cedar. In the hands of Odate's craftspeople, this fragrant wood is turned into the smoothest bento boxes, rice containers, trays and cups.

2.
Pottery
Down to earth

Japan has an exceptionally rich diversity of regional pottery styles: head to the rural village of Onta in Kyushu to find earthy Onta-ware that has been made the same way for 300 years or to Inbe for Bizen-ware, made from red, iron-rich clay. Pottery fans will find kilns clustered in places such as Mashiko in Tochigi, Karatsu in Saga and Yomitan in Okinawa. Each area's pottery is distinct and dependent on whatever the local soil provides.

3.
Lacquer
Extra coat

Once it hardens, the toxic sap of the Japanese *urushi* (lacquer tree) turns into a durable coating that can be applied to materials such as paper, metal and wood. Japanese lacquerware goes back thousands of years and ranges from soup bowls coated in clear lacquer to colour works by *maki-e* artists, including those in Kanazawa who use powdered gold or silver and mother-of-pearl to add decorative touches to lacquered pens, boxes and furniture.

4.
Enamelware
Weld and glaze

Japan excels at industrialised craft that requires a highly skilled workforce. Noda Horo, a family-owned company based in Tokyo and Tochigi prefecture, has been making enamel dishes since 1934. Steel plates are welded to make the basic shapes and the glaze is applied by hand, all in the company's small rural factories. The 60-strong company is run by Yasutomo Noda whose grandfather started the business.

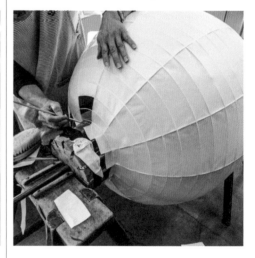

5.
Paper
Clean sheets

Washi is paper made in the traditional way from natural fibres. It's created in regions across Japan but the small town of Mino in Gifu prefecture is famous for paper handmade from *kozo* (mulberry) bark, which is textured and therefore leads to tougher paper. Today the area's famous *chochin* (paper lanterns) continue to be made with *washi* that's wrapped around a bamboo frame.

●

6.
Metalwork
Let it shine

Almost all of Japan's temple bells and statues are made in the city of Takaoka in Toyama, where craftsmen have been casting metal since the 17th century. Knife-making, a practice which descends from Japan's sword tradition, is centered around the city of Seki in Gifu. Over in Tsubame-Sanjo in Niigata, factories such as Yukiwa have made it the place to go for stainless-steel cutlery and kitchen equipment.

●

7.
Fabric
Material matters

The neighbourhood of Nishijin in Kyoto is the centre of the city's famed textile and weaving industry: many workshops and ateliers are creating kimono fabrics, hidden from public view. At Tatsumura Textile, weavers sit at looms making lustrous *obi* (kimono belts) and intricate pieces woven with peacock feathers to hang on festival floats. The company also painstakingly recreated the original hangings from the old Hotel Okura in Tokyo.

●

8.
Gold leaf
Finishing touch

Making *kin-paku* (gold leaf) involves pressing gold alloy into fragile sheets that are thinner than human hair. Production began in the late 16th century, when the use of *kin-paku* spread to Buddhist altars, Shinto shrines, lacquerware and textiles. Since the second half of the 19th century, workshops in the city of Kanazawa in Ishikawa prefecture have dominated the industry, producing radiant gold leaf that's also used in food, cosmetics and tableware.

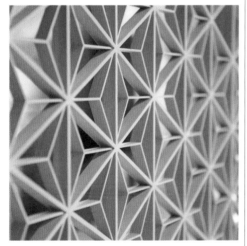

●

9.
Kumiko screens
All in the details

Japanese artisans have been making decorative wooden screens for centuries. The intricate patterns are created by hand using thousands of tiny pieces of wood – usually hinoki cypress – and no nails. Each of the 200 or so patterns has a different meaning. *Asanoha*, a geometric hemp leaf, is among the most popular and invokes longevity. For a good modern example of *kumiko* craftsmanship, head to the lobby of the new Okura Tokyo.

●

10.
Porcelain
Set in stone

The first Japanese porcelain was made in Arita on Kyushu island in the 17th century; the town is still lined with kilns and hosts a ceramics fair every spring. The early blues and whites gave way to a more colourful style referred to by European buyers as "Imari" after the Kyushu city from where porcelain was shipped. White Izushi-ware from the district of the same name in Hyogo prefecture is made from a local porcelain stone called *kakitani toseki*.

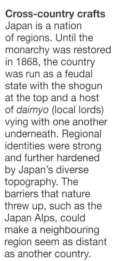

Cross-country crafts
Japan is a nation of regions. Until the monarchy was restored in 1868, the country was run as a feudal state with the shogun at the top and a host of *daimyo* (local lords) vying with one another underneath. Regional identities were strong and further hardened by Japan's diverse topography. The barriers that nature threw up, such as the Japan Alps, could make a neighbouring region seem as distant as another country.
    Nature played another role, providing the materials that forged regional crafts: trees for carpentry, clay for pottery and mulberry trees for paper. Families produced generations of craftspeople who followed their forebears and barely moved. There is much more mobility now of course, but those links with the past – long since dissolved in most industrialised countries – remain largely intact.
    Crafts have rarely strayed from where they first started: knives are still made in Seki (as swords once were), lacquer in Kanazawa and porcelain in Arita. The Japanese eyewear industry is concentrated in the town of Sabae in Fukui, where the industry began in 1905; the best craftsmen are still there (as are 95 per cent of the glasses made in Japan). The old feudal boundaries have disappeared but the country remains divided, today into its 47 prefectures – each of which has a clear view of its own identity.

Transport
モビリティ

4
四

How did we get here? It's a legitimate question that many travellers ask as they alight early for an appointment from sparkling bullet trains onto clean platforms. The rest of the world just doesn't seem to run like this.

Japan's world-leading transport industry – from cars to trains, trams and beyond – keeps the country moving and still has an edge over the global pack. The nation's obsession with speed and safety paid off – train and subway operators carry 25 billion passengers a year – but people and packages don't rely solely on tracks to get around.

In this chapter we explore forms of transport that are by turns practical and whimsical, from a battery-powered bicycle that's an urban family's essential ride to the first-class cabin aboard the ultra-fast Shinkansen. We also (politely) chase down police on bicycles and lunchtime noodle deliveries on mopeds. And when we're done, we hit an airport concourse where our editors are more than happy to while away some time in the – albeit unlikely – event of a delay. Let's move.

Trains:
On the right track

Trains can transform an economy and Japan's are a compelling case in point. High-speed Shinkansen whisk commuters between cities, cutting-edge stations spawn new communities and cleaning crews are held up as transport-sector heroes.

●

Shinkansen
Speed masters

Alfa-X sounds like something from the future and looks the part too. The ¥10bn (€82m) 10-car prototype Shinkansen has a long, flat nose cone at each end to quieten the boom as the train speeds through tunnels. It's a glimpse into the future of rail travel in Japan: the train will spend years in testing before it goes into service in 2031.

The long lead time to test a new Shinkansen might seem excessive but it's standard practice in a country where trains are vital to economic progress. When the first "bullet" trains debuted in 1964, the Shinkansen (meaning "new trunk line") ran along a single 515km-long line between Tokyo and Osaka. Today the trains whisk passengers at speeds topping 320km/h around a 3,100km-long national network. It's the world's busiest high-speed railway, with more than 130,000 train journeys a year running along the Tokyo-Osaka section, and yet the average delay is less than a minute.

A triumph of engineering and innovation, the Shinkansen has become a symbol of fast, efficient travel and a source of national pride. But the emphasis isn't only on speed; extraordinary service is part of the experience. With the introduction of Gran Class cars in 2011, trains have the luxe

option, with plush seats, a team of first-class attendants and dainty bento meals.

Improvements have been part of every new generation of trains. Hitachi, Kawasaki Heavy Industries and Nippon Sharyo among others have invested huge sums on trains that go faster, use less energy, ride more comfortably, make less noise and – when earthquakes hit – can brake suddenly without derailing. Careful planning and constant testing are reasons for the Shinkansen's unassailable

safety record: there has never been a major accident. And in a country frequently hammered by typhoons and earthquakes, only once has a Shinkansen derailed – in 2004 when a quake struck – but there were no casualties.

While the Alfa-X signifies a new chapter for the Shinkansen, Japan is pushing ahead with an even more ambitious project. By 2027 the country plans to launch its ultra-fast *maglev* (magnetic levitation) train, which is slated to travel at 500km/h.

Stations
Platform perfect

Railway stations in Japan are more than stops on train lines. They're gateways to regional tourism, promotional opportunities for local brands and gathering spots for residents. They entice visitors to linger and convey a unique sense of place.

This is what happens when railway operators grasp their potential: new communities spring up and remote places become attractive destinations, providing opportunities for entrepreneurs and producers to reach a new audience. Some stations have hot-spring foot spas and amusement parks for children, and many sell crafts and meals made with locally sourced ingredients.

Even at stations in faraway locales you come across retailers and restaurants that draw fans from afar. At JR Nagoya Station's platform, queues form for Sumiyoshi's *kishimen* (flat noodles) while Japanese saké aficionados rave about Ponshukan's tastings for 120 types of saké at Echigo-Yuzawa Station in Niigata.

Some stations are the work of renowned architects. Takaosanguchi Station, near the trails of Mount Takao, has an angled roof made from fragrant cedar that was designed by Kengo Kuma. In Hiroshima prefecture, Onomichi Station has undergone a transformation thanks to a tasteful expansion by Tokyo studio Atelier Bow-Wow in 2019. What was once a lonely outpost now has a diner serving fresh seafood from regional ports; a convenience store with travel essentials, newspapers and magazines; and a souvenir shop that specialises in products from Onomichi and the surrounding region.

Cleaning staff
Spic and span

The moment a Shinkansen pulls into Tokyo Station the clock starts ticking for the train's cleaning staff. The workers at JR East Tessei have just seven minutes to prepare a train with more than 1,000 seats for its next journey.

The job requires speed and precision because every Shinkansen spends only 12 minutes at the station. During holidays there can be as many as 180 trains a day that need cleaning. Once the arriving train is clear of passengers, Tessei's crew hop on, one person per car. In a flurry of activity they collect rubbish bags, turn the seats around, wipe down tables and windowsills, clean toilets and sinks, and sweep the aisles.

As they tidy, the staff keep an eye out for forgotten belongings on overhead shelves and seat pockets while inspectors walk through with thermal imaging machines looking for wet seat cushions. The final flourish is a bow to the awaiting queue of passengers – a gesture of hospitality and an apology of sorts for making them stand outside the train cars.

Keep it clean
Shinkansen cleaning crews take hospitality seriously. At Tokyo Station, both East Japan Railway and Central Japan Railway's cleaning staff bow to arriving and departing Shinkansen as well as queueing customers before and after tidying trains.

Bikes and boats:
Pedals and paddles

On Japan's waterways and city streets, boats and bicycles fill a gap where trains, planes and automobiles fall short. We've canvassed the country for good design and inspiring ideas.

◉

Mama-chari
Balancing act

The *mama-chari* (slang for "mama's bike") is the underrated workhorse of Japan's cities. These sturdy bicycles, designed with front and rear racks for baskets and child seats, have been around since the 1950s and are a popular choice for shuttling children to daycare and carting home bags of groceries. They're a guilt-free way of getting around and particularly practical in densely populated cities where parking spaces are hard to come by.

The latest hi-tech *mama-chari* models come with battery-powered pedal assist to help with steep inclines, thickly cushioned saddles, a low centre of gravity for stability and a price tag of roughly ¥130,000 (€1,000). Despite their name, *mama-chari* are not only for young mothers. You're just as likely to spot suited men, uniformed schoolchildren and retirees coasting by on these utilitarian two-wheelers.

◉

Engineered Bike Service
Hands on

With mass-market bike manufacturing now rooted in Taiwan and China, Japan's boutique brands are holding their own by appealing to a niche. One that reflects this small-scale approach is Engineered Bike Service (EBS), which began life in 2008 when expert bike builder Ryuji Sasaki (*pictured, on right*) and bike dealer Koji Kobayashi (*pictured, in centre*) started a workshop in Kyoto. "We make sports bikes but we also make utility bikes that can carry bags and children and are good for commuting," says Kobayashi.

The company's sleek, functional bikes have found a willing audience in customers who relish getting around on two wheels – and looking good while they're at it.

Keirin
Japan's love of fixed-gear bicycles has its roots in keirin racing. Steel-framed, single-speed keirin bicycles have been zipping around the country's velodrome tracks since 1948, when the sport was invented. These racing venues were the proving ground for a cottage industry of artisanal frame-making workshops whose handmade keirin bikes are now sought after by fashionable urbanites.

Tokyo Water Taxi

Inspired by the thriving boat traffic he'd seen in Sydney and Venice, Hajime Tabata – a former car engineer – decided to set up Tokyo's first water-taxi service. "Boats used to be Tokyo's main mode of transport but when cars and trains appeared the rivers became polluted and people lost interest in travelling along the river," he says. "Now the water is cleaner and the fish and birds are coming back. I felt sure there was scope to create a transport network along the waterways."

Launched in 2015, the company's yellow boats were custom-built in Yokosuka. Tabata negotiated with the city government to be able to stop at seven places around Tokyo and, by request, at 20 more piers, meaning his boats can reach as far as Tenkubashi to the south of the city. Tabata aims to eventually have a fleet of 60 boats and he's working with the city to improve signage to the piers.

⊙

Sano boats
Ship shape

"Our wooden boats often outlive the owners who commission them," says Ryutaro Sano, president of Sano Shipyard in Tokyo. The family business started in the early 1800s making wooden ships used for short journeys.

As demand for these vessels slowed, the family diversified into building boats and yachts to preserve the traditional craftsmanship. There is no shortcut to quality: a team of three designs and carves with traditional tools at their shipyard in Shiomi by Tokyo Bay. "It is great fun to create a ship from scratch," says Sano, who works with his brother Minoru and son Tatsuya. He favours Honduran mahogany for its supreme quality and burgundy sheen.

⊙

Sea Paseo
Favourite ferry

Around Japan's Seto Inland Sea, ferries are a lifeline connecting small islands to city ports. One ferry operator, Setonaikai Kisen, has reimagined its newest vessel – the Sea Paseo – as a notable tourist destination in its own right.

Launched in 2019, the Sea Paseo cuts a path through the island-dotted sea, stopping at Kure, Hiroshima and Matsuyama – three ports in Hiroshima and Ehime prefectures. As growing numbers of visitors find their way to this remote region, Setonaikai Kisen is counting on a bump in demand for premium ferry services.

The company hired Japan's GK Design Group to draw up plans for the 61-metre-long Sea Paseo, which has a stately blue-and-yellow livery, and can carry up to 35 cars and 300 passengers. Instead of the standard rows of seats, the ferry has sofas, stools, recliners and booths, as well as carpeted lounge areas where passengers can kick off their shoes and take in the view. On the upper decks are open patios and alfresco viewing areas with small gazebos that provide a shady place to sit.

Cars:
Behind the wheel

Japan's streets and highways are the backdrop for 81 million cars, vans, scooters and lorries. From micro-cars and stately chauffer-driven saloons to taxis painted a deep shade of indigo, the nation's automakers have designed and built the industry's transportation icons.

Toyota Century
Top drawer

Toyota's chauffeur-driven Century has been a favourite of Japanese politicians, CEOs and Imperial family members since its debut in 1967. The car has only been redesigned twice – most recently in 2018 – and Toyota has worked hard to preserve its classic blocky profile.

A few key upgrades make the ride more comfortable for the VIP in the backseat. The new Century has a quieter petrol-electric hybrid powertrain, a more spacious cabin, customised tyres for absorbing road shocks, and backseats with an improved massage function and footrests. There's an adjustable reading lamp and the lace curtains covering the rear window can be opened and closed with the touch-screen control panel.

Toyota only produces three of these cars a day at a factory in Japan where workers hand-chisel the hood emblem and delicately hammer out imperfections. The car's mirror-like paint job is both decorative and functional: getting out, a VIP can give his or her reflection a final once-over on the car body.

Name of the game
The Toyota Century is only available in the domestic market. It was named to honour the centenary of the birth of Sakichi Toyoda, founder of the Toyota Group.

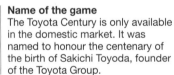

⦿ Suzuki Jimny
Squeeze in

For five decades, fans of the Suzuki Jimny have been drawn to its peerless combination of utility and personality. First released by the Japanese car-maker in 1970, it has sold 2.9 million units over four generations of models in more than 190 countries.

It's a compact four-wheel-drive and the precisely engineered mechanics of its chassis mean it's equally trusted by professionals rallying in Australian safari races as it is by mailmen delivering on winding roads in Japan's snowy regions. Then there are the aesthetics:

cute to some, cool to others. There's something appealing about a miniature version of an all-terrain car that's usually big and muscular. And no country is more fanatical about this micro-machine than Japan.

Twenty years on from the last new model, the fourth-generation Jimny was an overwhelming hit when it launched in 2018. Chief engineer Hiroyuki Yonezawa travelled through Japan, Europe and Africa to get feedback from users to understand the demands the next-generation vehicle would need to meet. Within a month of its release, orders had exceeded Suzuki's domestic annual sales target of 15,000 and the vehicle sold out globally.

⦿ JPN Taxi
All hail

They're hard to miss on the streets of Tokyo: bulbous taxis painted a deep indigo. Launched in late 2017, Toyota's JPN Taxi is a big improvement on the old, boxy model in every way. The rear door slides open automatically and the petrol-electric hybrid engine is both fuel-efficient and quiet. Thanks to a loftier roof and a low, flat floor, the

backseat is more comfortable for passengers – and spacious enough to fit a wheelchair.

Working closely with taxi company Nihon Kotsu, Toyota set out to create an instantly recognisable silhouette for an industry with a reputation for top-notch service. As taxi operators phase out their old cars, the JPN Taxi is taking over the country's fleet of 230,000.

On the street:
Take your pick

How Japan gets things done is closely connected to the movement of people and the logistics of businesses. Watch this to-ing and fro-ing play out on city streets, where vehicles are as much a part of the country's identity as food and drink.

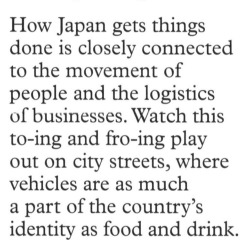

Planes:
Flights of fancy

For Japan, building aircraft is a chance to flex its engineering expertise and promote its national brand. It's an ambitious undertaking and a logical next step for a country with a reputation for setting high hospitality standards in the air travel industry.

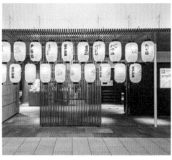

Mitsubishi SpaceJet M90
Made in Japan

Designed and built on home turf by Mitsubishi Aircraft Corporation, the SpaceJet M90, unveiled in 2019, is Japan's first commercial aeroplane in half a century – and the country's second-ever postwar production of a passenger plane in Japan.

The aircraft has been a long time coming: after delays, design issues, slow orders and strong market scepticism, the SpaceJet was subject to a decade-long development phase that has cost hundreds of billions of yen (billions of euros). The model offers more space than previous regional planes while also promising better fuel-efficiency than other aircraft of a similar size.

Haneda Airport
Retail departure

When Tokyo's Haneda Airport opened its new international terminal in 2010, travellers rejoiced. The retail centrepiece of its departure building, Edo Koji, is a replica of a historical Japanese town. Along the recreated streets of Edo (Tokyo's ancient name), "Made in Japan" shops include Tokyo-based beauty brand Makanai Cosme. Restaurants include Ariso Sushi, Katsusen for *tonkatsu* (deep-fried pork cutlet) and *sukiyaki* (simmered beef) specialist Takafuku, while one floor up is Tokyo Pop Town, home to anime and toys.

Inflight food
Since 2011, Japan Airlines has collaborated with restaurants to make tasty comfort food: Yoshinoya beef bowls, Mos Burger teriyaki burgers and Shiseido Parlour quiches. It's an art replicating flavours for the harsh plane environment.

All Nippon Airways uniforms
Look sharp

Flight attendants are the brand ambassadors of any airline and those at All Nippon Airways (ANA) wear their colours with panache. Their uniforms – in shades of blue, grey and pink – combine a well-tailored silhouette with a playful element: a two-toned blue stripe down each sleeve of the jacket, and down the back of skirts for women, and floral-patterned scarves that add an understated flourish.

ANA hired Nepalese-American fashion designer Prabal Gurung – known for dressing royalty and pop stars – to create outfits for 13,000 of the airline's staff that would modernise their look while staying true to the brand's signature colours. Even with the limited palette, Gurung came up with a solution that is both unifying but also shuns monotony by giving staff the option of different coloured shirts and scarves to go with light grey jackets and charcoal skirts or trousers. The uniforms are an instant classic befitting Japan's largest airline.

Test the waters
Setouchi Seaplanes is Japan's first airline to rely on amphibious aircraft in half a century. The company's fleet includes a plane with a red livery that was designed by anime director Hayao Miyazaki's Studio Ghibli.

Setouchi Seaplanes
View from above

The idea to launch Setouchi Seaplanes was straightforward: promote tourism around the Seto Inland Sea region by giving visitors a bird's-eye view of it. The company – formed as part of a broader initiative to raise the profile of the western port city of Onomichi – now operates three Kodiak propeller planes, with a logo and livery by graphic designer Naomi Hirabayashi. It runs the country's only commercial flight services that take off and land on water.

At Setouchi Seaplanes' main base on a wharf in Onomichi, a lounge overlooks the water. Thousands of passengers have come through here mainly for flights over and around Shodoshima and other islands.

With a new permit to use Hiroshima Airport in 2020, the company is expanding the range of its chartered flights. It also uses a wharf in Matsue city, Shimane prefecture, to complement its base in Onomichi, and has been approached by other municipalities with similar hopes of luring visitors.

Business
ビジネス

5
五

Though different in scale and scope, all the Japanese businesses we feature here have a few things in common. Some question the norm and cultivate unconventional ideas while others undertake services you'd never find in Europe or the US. All understand that whether you're running a vast logistics firm in a city or a tiny family-owned furniture brand in the hinterlands, attention to detail and sharp service still matter.

The folks you'll meet on the following pages know that hitting targets and pleasing investors is one thing – this is the world's third-largest economy, after all. But many also spare a thought for the long game: looking after staff, investing in the community and keeping craft alive are important. Some businesses hope to preserve traditions while others have cottoned on to the fact that a niche product can appeal to the masses. In each case, there's a belief that their work can improve the lives of their customers – something the world can learn from.

Business success stories:
In good company

All great businesses start with an idea. The companies featured here are benchmarks in their particular fields, whether that's rethinking how we live, furnishing a community or capturing the nation's imagination with a cuddly black bear.

⬤
Yamagata Design
Pushing for a rural return

Yamagata Design is on a mission to revitalise northern Japan's vast Shonai Plain. This fertile sweep of land in Yamagata prefecture is home to some of the country's best rice fields but also, like many other rural areas, subject to alarming levels of depopulation.

Before 2013, Tokyo-born founder Daisuke Yamanaka was busy climbing the career ladder at Mitsui Fudosan, one of Japan's largest developers. "I worked on many big projects. But one day it occurred to me: 'Do we need any more shopping centres in our country?'" he says. "I decided to do something that serves society more."

Yamanaka quit his job in 2014 and, with an initial investment of just ¥100,000 (€830), Yamagata Design was born. His first project was Suiden Terrasse. He commissioned award-winning architect Shigeru Ban and by summer 2018 the 143-room hotel was open. A low-rise complex that seemingly floats above the waterlogged fields surrounding it, the hotel has a farm-to-table restaurant, a hot spring, a library space and a shop selling crafts.

Next door he has opened an innovative children's centre, Kids Dome Sorai. Also designed by Ban and constructed mainly from natural materials, it features a long sloped terrain with a six-metre-high rope-climbing structure, as well as a spacious workshop with plenty of materials and tools for arts and crafts. The idea is to make the area more attractive for young families thinking about relocating.

Although there is no perfect recipe for rural regeneration, Yamanaka shows that it can be done. The company he started solo now employs 70 full-time staff. Half of them moved or returned to Shonai. "People tend to think the top talent are overqualified to work in places like this but the opposite is true," he says. "We live in a time where we need those people to challenge themselves in rural areas."

⬤
Bake
Promoting one-product shops

Founded in 2013, Japanese confectionery company Bake is shaking up the market with a unique business strategy: one-product shops known for their sleek, minimalist design. Each of its seven "brands" has its own name: Ringo is for apple pies, Press Butter Sand is for biscuits and so on. "It's not that we can only do one thing but we choose to do that one thing," says Bake's designer Seiji Sadakiyo. "This strategy has allowed us to invest in quality ingredients, tailor shop as well as package design, and have fresh on-site baking operations."

Nothing here has been left to chance: everything from the pared-back interiors, chic logo and clever packaging has been fine-tuned by Sadakiyo and partner art director Hiroko Shiratori. "Lots of our staff come from the fashion industry," says Sadakiyo. "Others are from consulting, automobile and financial markets."

Its simplified approach to bricks-and-mortar retail has seen Bake build a unique brand in a saturated market. "If you look at winning companies such as Apple and Dyson, their design is beautiful," he says. "We notice that this is happening in the food industry too."

Muji House
Redefining the Japanese home

Muji aims to address one of the biggest problems with homes in Japan: they are often not comfortable to live in. "The idea that your entire house should be warm in winter and cool in summer exists in the West but not in Japan," says Koji Kawachi, the director and head architect of Muji House, the brand unit that has been designing and selling homes since 2004.

Muji sells four types of homes. They differ in shape and layout but all share the spare, functional aesthetic of the homeware, stationery and button-down shirts that the brand is more widely known for. The standard Muji House comes with extra insulation and triple-paned windows, as well as a sturdy frame that meets Japan's highest quake-resistance standards and maintains a comfortable temperature across the seasons.

Another aim of Muji House is to address the scrap-and-build cycle in Japan by providing houses with longevity. It's an ambitious agenda for a company that builds just 300 homes a year, compared with the 10,000 to 25,000 of the country's largest builders. "We're small but expanding," says Kawachi. "It shows there's a lot of potential."

In Nagoya, at one of Muji's 32 model-home locations in Japan, MONOCLE meets prospective buyers Toshihiro and Sayuri Hiei. The couple have driven nearly an hour because Sayuri is a fan of the brand. "I like the simplicity but I haven't heard enough about the features to make a decision," says Sayuri. Unlike rivals, Muji doesn't upsell or haggle. Its houses even sport physical price tags: a two-storey house costs ¥20m (€153,000).

Nagoya is also home to Takeshi and Mizuho Maki who, along with their son, have lived in a Muji Window House for several years. They were drawn to Muji House by its clean designs; most of their possessions are stashed away in cabinets built into the walls. But could a Muji House be too plain? "Think of a house as a cake," says Takeshi. "When you're given a white cake you can choose how to decorate it. If it comes already decorated, it can get in the way of your plans."

Muji
If Muji doesn't have it, do you really need it? The store started out in 1980 as the in-house brand for retailer Seiyu. Today the shelves of its 900-odd outlets worldwide are stacked with everything from slippers to suitcases, all created by Japan's best and brightest design talent. The brand has also expanded over the years to encompass a range of different services, including hotels, cafés and bookshops.

Kumamon
Capturing the nation's imagination

Like most Japanese public servants, Kumamon has a desk, business cards and demure work attire. At the Kumamoto prefectural government in western Japan he juggles two senior roles, as director of both the sales and the happiness divisions. The difference between Kumamon and other prefecture employees is that he is wide-eyed and rosy cheeked, with a body that recalls a chubby black bear. He is also the official mascot and quite the celebrity.

Tourists come from overseas to see him and companies around the country jump at the chance to put his image on their products. On a weekday afternoon you'll find him in his office in downtown Kumamoto. This is where his fans come for hugs and high fives.

Kumamon first appeared in 2010 to promote a new Shinkansen line cutting through this mostly agricultural region of 1.7 million residents. It was designer Manabu Mizuno's idea to create a mascot for the campaign. "The prefecture asked for a logo but I was sceptical that a logo would stand out. I thought it would be good to have someone doing Kumamoto's PR," says Mizuno, who heads the Tokyo-based Good Design Company.

Around Kumamoto you can't escape Kumamon. He's on buses, billboards, vending machines, bicycles, cakes, hotel-room bedding and aeroplanes. He's collaborated on limited-offer products with Mini, Baccarat, Leica and Steiff. The most diehard Kumamon enthusiasts spend their holidays shadowing him at events around Japan. His annual fan gatherings in Osaka and Tokyo, and a birthday celebration in Kumamoto every March, collectively draw tens of thousands of people. He once greeted Japan's emperor and empress, and he raised ¥3.6m (€30,000) partly through an online campaign to help fund repairs to Notre Dame cathedral in Paris after it was devastated by fire.

Kumamoto officials grasped early on how social media could magnify their message and sent Kumamon to Osaka for an experiment in viral marketing. He would turn up without warning and without any indication of what he was there for. By the time Kumamoto officials volunteered an explanation, Kumamon was an online sensation.

Kumamon might not have been so ubiquitous if it hadn't been for the prefecture's Harvard-educated governor, Ikuo Kabashima. He had the idea of licensing Kumamon's image to businesses for free as long as they adhered to certain rules. So many businesses have come knocking since then that the prefecture has had to outsource the work of approving applications from licensees.

Uniqlo
Chanelling the everyday

"When we say 'everyday clothes for everyday people' it sounds mundane but it's a deep thing for us," says Uniqlo's president of global creative John C Jay. Selling everything from multi-packs of vests and thermal leggings to big-name collaborations from the likes of Jil Sander and Alexander Wang, the brand has made a name for itself as a purveyor of high-quality wardrobe staples at high-street prices.

The first branch of Uniqlo – or Unique Clothing Warehouse – opened its doors in Hiroshima in 1984 and has since grown to become a global business with more than 2,200 shops worldwide. The brand was born when owner Tadashi Yanai inherited a clothing shop from his father; today Yanai is president of the largest clothing retailer in Asia, Fast Retailing, and the richest person in Japan. Alongside Uniqlo, the group also owns Helmut Lang, Theory and J Brand, and has annual sales of more than ¥2trn (€16.5bn).

The art of 'meishi'

Rule number one of doing business in Japan: always carry a stack of *meishi* (business cards). Exchanging *meishi* is the first thing you do when meeting anyone unfamiliar and it's not taken lightly. The rules and rituals aren't that complicated – they just take a little practice.

Do:
Exchange cards with the most senior person in the room first and most junior person last. If someone of a higher rank from your company is present, let them go first.

Take one at a time from the card case.

Using both hands, offer your card – letters up for the recipient – while introducing yourself and your company. Presenting your card on a card case is common but not essential.

When exchanging cards with a senior-ranking person, wait until that person lets go before you do. Release your card one hand at a time, left first. Wait to release your right until after the other person has accepted it. Bow slightly from the waist.

Spend a moment looking at the card. It's polite to comment on the *kanji* (characters) of the person's name, the paper stock or the company's address.

During the meeting, place the cards you've received in front of you or on top of your card case. If there are several cards, arrange them in front of you. Keep them there until the meeting ends.

Don't:
Exchange cards across a tabletop.

Pull your card from a pocket or put the other person's card into your pocket.

Use cards with worn edges or stains.

Put the card away until the end of the meeting.

Use cards for origami.

Yamatomichi
Climbing every mountain

Akira and Yumiko Natsume quit their Tokyo office jobs and started ultra-lightweight mountaineering brand Yamatomichi in 2011 so they could spend more time on trails. The couple's speciality is in ultralight hiking gear: backpacks, sleeping mats and clothes that they design at their office-atelier-shop in Kamakura, a beach town southwest of Tokyo. "Ultralight hiking isn't only about carrying less weight, it's a way of thinking and a skill." says Akira. "How do you make do with as little as possible?"

Since launching their first product – a foam sleeping mat that was a third of the weight of those made by their Japanese rivals – the Natsumes have added to their line-up items that they wanted for themselves but couldn't find. They rely on trial and error to optimise their products for Japan's wet and windy climate and rugged terrain. "We might spend a year or two – sometimes three or four – taking a prototype such as a backpack into the mountains and we make small improvements until we are satisfied," says Akira.

They have drawn on their own mishaps for inspiration. During one trip, Yumiko fell and tore the shoulder strap of her backpack, which led the couple to come up with a sturdier design. Another time, Akira was caught in an unexpected snowstorm and kept himself warm by adding layers around his midriff. "We thought a lot about where to put pockets on jackets," he says. "You can put anything in your pockets for insulation and wind-protection."

They're doing something right: it took just two years for Yamatomichi to become profitable. Today their products, made in small batches of several hundred to 1,000 items at a time, sell out within days of release.

Lawson
Keeping it convenient

Anyone who has ever been to a Lawson will immediately grasp the possibilities of Japan's 24-hour *konbini* (convenience stores). At any of the 55,600 that exist in the country, you can pay your taxes or utilities bills, withdraw cash, send packages and buy concert tickets. If you're looking for stationery, snacks or saké, or necessities such as socks and soap, you'll find them all here. And the selection of edibles is constantly changing: food and drink brands use *konbini* as a crucial testing ground for their newest, seasonal products.

Japan's top three *konbini* chains are 7-Eleven, FamilyMart and Lawson. The industry's third-largest, Lawson has 14,600 stores that have become a fixture of downtown neighbourhoods, suburbs, train stations, highway rest stops and government office buildings, and serve an increasingly vital role in communities that have no nearby supermarkets. Its annual revenue tops ¥2.4trn (€20bn) and the concept continues to evolve.

Several shops feature over-the-counter drugs and a 24-hour hotline to a pharmacist, and in 2001 the company launched the first of its Natural Lawson stores, specialising in low-calorie boxed meals, additive-free drinks and eco-friendly beauty products. *Konbini* have even become a lifeline for disaster-hit areas providing vital food and supplies.

Yamato postal service
Delivering parcels like no other

In Japan's parcel-delivery business, Yamato Transport is a heavyweight. Founded in 1919 as a chartered lorry service, the Tokyo-based company delivers 1.8 billion packages – roughly 44 per cent of the domestic total – and 1.4 billion pieces of mail annually.

So ubiquitous are Yamato's black cat logo and tan-and-green-uniformed couriers that the company's *takkyubin* (delivery) service has become a generic term for sending packages. You can send your suitcase ahead to the airport, your unwieldy golf and ski equipment to the slopes, and even a chilled wagyu steak to your relatives.

Lately the company has put its domestic network of 60,000 drivers and 4,000 offices to use delivering groceries to homes in remote areas with no nearby supermarket, checking on elderly residents and organising aid shipments when disasters hit. To replicate its model across Asia, Yamato has turned to a hi-tech logistics system that can figure out the fastest route by air, land and sea, speed containers through customs and organise the complex handoff at airports and harbours.

The company is already demonstrating its astonishing efficiency across borders, delivering, say, sea urchin caught off the coast of Aomori to hotels and restaurants in Hong Kong in time for dinner the following evening. But it's also focusing on service: since moving into Shanghai and Singapore in 2010, Yamato has built local centres to train the army of polite, uniformed drivers who are the face of the brand – a major reason for its success in Japan.

Ishinomaki Laboratory
Rebuilding a community

When the northeast coast of Japan was struck by a devastating earthquake and tsunami in 2011, the city of Ishinomaki was among the hardest hit. One project that emerged from the wreckage was Ishinomaki Laboratory, a furniture workshop founded by architect Keiji Ashizawa to help rebuild the shattered community.

When US furniture manufacturer Herman Miller got involved the idea developed further. The team opened a community space and renovated a small bar – somewhere for volunteers and locals to relax. They also started making simple stools for people living in temporary homes and the Ishinomaki Laboratory brand was born.

Their work might have continued as a welcome but under-the-radar project had Ashizawa not come up with a couple of outstanding designs: the Ishinomaki Bench, made for the temporary outdoor cinema; and the Ishinomaki Stool, which is on its way to becoming a Japanese design classic. This sturdy piece is assembled from a flat-pack with a hammer and a few nails – and is so simple it can be made by anyone.

Moonstar
Shodding the nation

Founded in 1873 as a custom-maker of cloth split-toe tabi socks, Moonstar began producing rubber in the 1920s and, soon afterwards, rubber-soled footwear. The company's shoe empire expanded until rising production costs became a threat to growth. By 2000, Moonstar had shifted most of its production to factories overseas to cut costs. Designer Kenta Matsunaga and three other young colleagues worried that the Kurume factory's days were numbered and devised a plan to save it.

In 2010 they designed a shoe with a vulcanised rubber sole (calling it Shoes Like Pottery because of the baking) for an exhibition about the manufacturing process. "It was just supposed to be a storytelling tool," he says. Yet so many people asked about it that Matsunaga's team persuaded Moonstar's higher-ups to launch Shoes Like Pottery a year later.

Today nearly 90 lifestyle shops and fashion retailers around Japan (and some overseas) sell their shoes, all of which are designed in-house and made in a factory at the headquarters in Kurume. "The rubber comes from Moonstar's own facility next door," says factory manager Kiyoteru Takahara.

Meet the people
人々

Japan is home to some 127 million people – a vast number that doesn't reveal much about the changing nation's nuances, charm and pluck. Over the years, MONOCLE has met countless artists, chefs, gardeners, taxi drivers, salarymen and stationmasters, both in big cities and remote corners. In this chapter we present portraits of people with whom we've shared fond memories – some well-known, others less so, all representing modest but meaningful roles in the national story.

You'll meet firefighters, property tycoons and coastguard recruits, as well as national treasures, a karate kid and a celebrity canine with a winning smile (you'll see what we mean). What do they all have in common? Their dogged pursuit of perfection in all manner of endeavours; efforts that have in some small way shaped and contributed to the nation we adore and also helped reimagine it abroad. Come and meet them – it's time to get a bit personal.

Mahiro Takano
Karate champion
Mahiro Takano from the Niigata city of Nagaoka looks
like an ordinary teenager. But once she puts on her kit
she becomes a dazzling national champion of Shotokan
Karate kata, a sequence of moves. The teen prodigy started
karate when she was four, encouraged by the master who
was teaching her older brother. Within two years she was a
black belt and she won the primary-school category at the
national championships for six consecutive years.

Photographed at the Miyamoto Community Centre, Nagaoka

205

Morihide Yoshida
Patissier
Morihide Yoshida relocated
to Paris from Japan in 2010
and launched his celebrated
patisserie three years later.
At his sleek boutique in the
seventh arrondissement, glass
cabinets are filled with the crème
de la crème of classic French
baking, from flaky croissants
to chocolate-praline desserts.
"French customers expect me
to inject a Japanese twist into
my pastries but that's not what
brought me to Paris," he says.
"I came here to work with fine
French ingredients that I didn't
have access to in Japan."

Photographed at Abri Soba,
a restaurant in Paris

Maru
Model
Japan is a nation of dog lovers,
with about nine million mutts
at the last count. The dogs are as
diverse a bunch as their owners:
large and small; fluffy and
short-haired; some transported
in prams and bike baskets; some
dressed in clothes. Aside from
the overwhelming number of
mini pedigree pooches, Japan
has six native breeds: the Shiba,
Akita, Kai, Kishu, Shikoku and
Hokkaido. Maru here is a shiba –
a dog known for its intelligence,
bravery and loyalty – and a
nationwide star with a busy
modelling career and 2.5 million
followers on Instagram.

Photographed at Nezu Shrine, Tokyo

Coastguard recruits
At the Japan Coast Guard
Academy in Kure, Hiroshima
prefecture, men and women
are trained in everything from
diving, shooting and kendo to
international law, mathematics
and meteorology. They spend
four years in the classroom,
another six months working
in a specialised area and a
further three months journeying
around the world on a training
ship. At the end of it all, 40
graduates emerge each year
with a degree and their first
assignment aboard a patrol
vessel as a junior-grade officer.

Academy students photographed
taking part in cutter training in Kure

Tokyo Metropolitan Park Association

The Tokyo Metropolitan Park Association manages and maintains 46 parks, nine gardens, eight cemeteries and a crematorium, as well as harbour and river ferry services. Executive director Katsuhiko Sano leads a team of specialists who design parks, heal trees and keep a close eye on the city's biodiversity. The team also includes history experts who know all there is to know about feudal-era falconry and duck-hunting, sales staff who develop new sweets for concession stands, and experienced horticulturalists putting young gardeners through rigorous technical programmes.

Photographed at Hamarikyu Gardens, Tokyo

Fire brigade volunteer

The *shobodanin* are volunteer firefighters in the shape of a community force that backs up Japan's regular fire brigade. They do anything from checking on elderly residents to wielding a fire hose and have even been known to deliver aid on motorbikes and travel on jet-skis through flooded areas. There are 844,000 of them up and down Japan. By day they are salarymen, housewives, grocers and shopkeepers; out of hours they are arranged in 2,200 units around the country.

Photographed in Daizawa, Tokyo

Jun Tada
Udon taxi driver

In Kagawa prefecture, Sanuki udon is comfort food (Sanuki is the ancient provincial name). It's cheap and simple fare: you slurp it down with fish broth or soy sauce and the toppings – ginger, green onions, raw egg or tempura – of your choice. Udon is a big draw for tourists and Jun Tada is the guide to call on. As an udon taxi driver for transport company Kotohira Bus, Tada takes visitors to small, hard-to-find shops while treating them to the dish's entertaining cultural backstory.

Photographed near the Doki river in Marugame city, Kagawa prefecture

Stationmaster

It's not hard to grasp what elevates the best of Japan's train stations: the stationmaster. These experienced professionals on the railway industry's front lines are hospitality experts who lead by example. You might find them sweeping platforms, retrieving items dropped on the tracks or helping stranded passengers during delays. They're familiar with the timetable and put safety – for commuters, schoolchildren, seniors and tourists – first.

Photographed at Onomichi Station

Miwako Date
CEO

A female executive in a sector that's dominated by conservative middle-aged men, Miwako Date is the dynamic CEO of Mori Trust. She oversees a multibillion-euro portfolio, with 24 hotels and resorts, roughly 100 office buildings and residences, and annual revenue of ¥175bn (€1.4bn). Since taking over from her father in 2016, Date has been cajoling officials into loosening restrictive rules while persuading the likes of Hilton Worldwide, Shangri-La Hotels and Resorts and Marriott to bet on the Japanese market.

Photographed at the Conrad Tokyo hotel

Milet
Singer
The husky voice of singer-songwriter Milet has been a growing presence on Japanese airwaves. The Tokyo talent, who only began focusing on music full-time in 2018, released her debut EP *Inside You* in March 2019. The title track, also used as the theme for television drama *Queen*, topped the charts on a host of streaming services, propelling her into the spotlight.

Photographed at Bunkamura recording studio, Tokyo

Sayaka Murata
Writer
Novelist Sayaka Murata joined some of the biggest names in Japanese literature when she won the Akutagawa prize in 2016 for *Conbini Ningen* (*Convenience Store Woman*), a cool dissection of the dysfunction of Japanese society as seen through the eyes of a convenience-store worker. A rare international hit for a Japanese writer, it has been translated into 30 languages.

Photographed in Ladrio café, Tokyo

Hospitality
おもてなし

7

七

Drinking, dining and hotels are rightly among Japan's greatest strengths. From five-star stays to rural retreats and luxury ryokans, the island nation has refined the art of hospitality in ways that the world could learn a lot from.

Technology can play a role but humanity, care and kindness shine through in the best establishments. Whether it's a drip coffee in an age-old *kissaten* (coffee shop) or a highball in a smart lobby bar, there's a level of service that's genuine, personal and persists throughout the country.

This is all before we sit down at a table to sample the dishes that have made Japan a world leader in food and drink. From traditional *tonkatsu* (deep-fried pork cutlet) joints and lively izakaya pubs to neighbourhood noodle bars and delicate *kaiseki* (multi-course) cookery, there are plenty of secrets we're keen to reveal.

Eating:
Food on the table

The ways in which you can eat in Japan are as diverse as the range of food you can order. From casual izakaya to counter dining and smart establishments, the restaurant scene is delightfully rich and colourful.

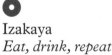

Izakaya
Eat, drink, repeat

A visit to an izakaya (a Japanese pub) reveals a great deal about how people in Japan eat out. This is where hardworking residents come to kick back after a long day at the office.

Each izakaya has its own speciality, from seafood to chicken. Locals tuck into unfussy dishes such as edamame beans, pickled vegetables, sashimi and *kara-age* (deep-fried chicken) – basically anything that pairs well with a drink. Speaking of which, there will be round after round of Asahi and Sapporo, as well as *umeshu* (plum wine) and highballs.

It's a convivial set-up, with groups sitting around a table ordering plates to share. And if you fancy something smarter, there are more upmarket independent types as well as chains.

Burger and pizza joints
Topping the list

Burgers and pizzas aren't the obvious foods associated with Japan but, believe it or not, the country is home to some of the best in the business. Think about Japanese tailors and shoemakers, who elevate their trade to another dimension by honing their skills in Naples or Northampton and then adding their own twist. Well, restaurateurs and chefs strive for this perfection too.

Places such as Golden Brown (*pictured*) and The Great Burger in Tokyo make mouthwatering gourmet wagyu burgers, while popular neighbourhood chain Mos Burger fills its buns with lots of high-quality Japanese ingredients. Hisanori Yamamoto at Pizzeria e trattoria da Isa in Nakameguro in Tokyo is a world pizza champion, while Pizza Slice (*pictured*) has perfected the authentic New York style.

Counter dining
Pull up a stool

"Chef's table" may be a recently coined term but Japan has always had a culture of counter dining. And it's not just casual noodle dishes such as udon and ramen. Traditional Japanese food from tempura to sushi has long been served and eaten at the counter.

Customers get a good view of the ingredients, which are neatly laid out in spotless glass display cabinets, as well as all the action, from razor-sharp knife skills to delicate plating. In close proximity, chef and customers enjoy conversation that simply isn't possible in a regular restaurant setting.

Sushi Takigawa (*pictured*), an eight-seater sushi restaurant in Fukuoka, is just one example of counter dining in Japan. The interior is refreshingly minimal, allowing diners to enjoy the theatre of watching a skilled chef prepare and serve quality sushi before their eyes.

⬤ Udon shops
Oodles of noodles

These thick, white noodles are a speciality of Kagawa prefecture in southwest Japan. Made from wheat flour, water and salt, they're an expression of the region's climate, which is sunny and dry – ill-suited to rice but ideal for wheat. Salt producers dot the coast and the fishing fleets of nearby Ibukijima island catch the baby sardines that are dried for the broth.

In Kagawa, udon is a cheap and cheerful staple that's served quickly without much fancy flavouring. It works as a meal or a snack and there's no elegant way to eat it: just slurp noisily and cut the noodles with your teeth. Aficionados even talk about *nodo-goshi*, the sensation of noodles slithering down your throat.

To achieve *koshi* (the springy-firm texture), noodle-makers work long shifts. "We make dough the night before so it can rest for hours," says Mitoe Miyagawa, the second-generation owner of Miyagawa Seimenjo in Zentsuji city. In the morning, while the broth is cooking, she and her husband Masaru pack the dough into balls that are then stomped flat with their feet, rolled thin and cut into noodles. Their two daughters are in charge of boiling and cold-rinsing.

Shops open at sunrise for early risers and keep their doors open for the late-night crowd. Kagawa's 700 or so udon shops outnumber its convenience stores; no other prefecture has more per capita. The noodle is so ubiquitous here that Kagawa has branded itself the udon prefecture. Taxi and bus operators lead udon tours, udon schools host seminars and udon mascots are local stars.

Family restaurants
The kids are alright

Known as *fami resu*, family restaurants are an unmissable feature of the Japanese dining scene. They first appeared in 1970 when a Royal restaurant – predecessor to Royal Host – popped up at the Osaka Expo and dished out 2,000 Hamburg steaks (*see page 227*) a day. In 1971 the first Royal Host outpost opened in Kitakyushu, Fukuoka, with the help of the Hotel New Grand in Yokohama, where *yoshoku* (Japanese-style western food) was pioneered.

Today the *fami resu* industry – with chains such as Denny's, Joyfull and Jonathan's (*pictured*) – has grown to ¥1.3trn (€10.6bn). Among the leaders is Skylark Group, whose Jonathan, Bamiyan and Gusto chains are part of a 3,200-restaurant empire. The winning formula? A car park for convenience; a child-friendly menu of pilaf, pancakes and ginger pork; and long opening hours. You don't have to be with a family to feel at home; solo customers are welcome too.

Tempura restaurants
Small fry

Japan has Portugal to thank for its tempura – those crisply fried, delicately flavoured fresh seafood and vegetables we adore. The origin of its cooking method goes back to the 16th century when missionaries from Portugal introduced the Japanese to religious ceremonies called *temporas*, which involved the Catholics eating fried fish and vegetables. A century later, in the Edo period, tempura was available at street-food stands along with sushi, soba noodles and *unagi* (eel).

The Japanese have perfected the craft and today need-to-impress client meetings happen at some of the finest tempura restaurants. Seasoned chefs get so close to the heated oil that they almost dip their fingers in.

Ekiben

After a few days in Japan, many visitors from overseas notice that Japanese people don't eat while walking on the street. But they do eat when travelling.

Ekiben – a word that stems from *eki* (station) and bento – is a fine example of how seriously food is taken in this country. Each meal is not only about meeting daily nutritional needs but also pure and simple enjoyment.

Ekiben come in all shapes and sizes, many of which feature local specialities and seasonings. Tokyo Station offers the greatest inventory of *ekiben*, which are sent daily from across the country. Everything from *makunouchi* (the most classic bento box, with plain rice and an assortment of side dishes) to a Hokkaido seafood special is beautifully prepared and wrapped.

Oh, and when you see steam swirling up from someone's seat on a train, fear not. Your neighbour has just pulled the cord of their beef bento – a self-heating version, which heats up in minutes to an appetising temperature.

So take your pick then take a seat. After all, what better way is there to explore the country's diverse food culture than while travelling by Shinkansen?

What to order:
Pick and choose

Ready for a food marathon? From sushi and soba to sweet buns and shortcake, Japanese movers and shakers have perfected their menu. Here's a taster.

Sushi
Fish, rice and vinegar is the simplest combination and yet not the easiest to pull off. It's embedded in daily life and available everywhere from supermarkets to starry restaurants.

Makunouchi bento
The classic bento lunch box consists of plain rice and an assortment of colourful side dishes including grilled fish, meat and vegetables.

Sanma-no-shioyaki
Grilled fish such as *sanma* (Pacific saury) is a popular lunch option. The typical set is a bargain and includes rice, miso soup and pickles.

Crab-cream croquette
Korokke (croquettes) filled with *kani* (crab) cream are a standard feature of *yoshoku* (Japanese-style western food) restaurants and casual izakaya.

Takoyaki
Originally from Osaka, *takoyaki* (octopus balls) are a popular street snack in Japan. Seasoned with sauce, mayonnaise, powdered seaweed and bonito flakes.

Wagyu steak
Japan has many wagyu beef brands but Kobe, Matsusaka, Omi and Yonezawa are the big four. Some are widely distributed while others are rare.

Oden
A popular winter hotpot with seafood, vegetables and eggs. It's perfect for home parties but there are *oden* restaurants too. Regional variations apply.

Tempura
Perfect tempura – made with fish, prawns and seasonal vegetables – is light in oil but rich in flavour. Dip it in sauce (soy, mirin or dashi) or sprinkle with salt.

Katsu Sando
The *tonkatsu* (deep-fried pork cutlet) sandwich was invented at *tonkatsu* restaurant Isen in Tokyo in 1935. The bread was thinly sliced so it wouldn't ruin a geisha's lipstick.

Omuraisu
Ketchup-flavoured rice wrapped in an omelette topped with extra ketchup. Popular with everyone from children to the elderly, and eaten both out and at home.

Gyoza
Dumplings filled with ground pork, chopped cabbage, leek and garlic, and wrapped in dough. Crispy outside and juicy in the middle, these are a beer's best friend.

Onigiri
This rice ball wrapped in seaweed is an equivalent to western sandwiches. Convenience stores have a huge inventory, from plain salt to fillings of salmon or *umeboshi* (sour plum).

Zaru soba
A cold soba noodle dish that's popular in summer. Served on a *zaru* (bamboo strainer), topped with a sprinkle of seaweed and with dipping sauce and grated wasabi.

Yakitori
Literally translated as "grilled chicken", *yakitori* includes all parts of a chicken – from the skin to the heart – which are skewered and grilled with vegetables over charcoal.

Ramen
Soy sauce, salt, miso and *tonkotsu* (pork-bone broth) – there are many styles of ramen. People eat it for lunch, dinner and after a night out, and it ranges from cheap to gourmet.

Hamburg steak with Napolitan
Japanese people grow up eating juicy, mouthwatering Hamburg steak. It's a fixture at family restaurants and sometimes served with spaghetti – a winning combo.

Nabe
A *nabe* (hotpot) is great for a gathering of families or friends. Common ingredients include tofu, shiitake mushrooms and chicken but there are myriad varieties.

Western-style Japanese breakfast
Yoshoku (Japanese-style western) breakfast at a hotel in Japan features fried eggs with ham, mini sausages, a small salad and the thickest and fluffiest of toast.

Fruit parfait
A classic treat in old-school fruit parlours. Strawberry, melon, mango, chocolate and ice cream – the possibilities are endless.

Melon pan
A Japanese sweet bun that doesn't taste like melon but supposedly looks like one. The best are crunchy outside and fluffy inside. Tokyo's Kagetsudo is an institution.

Baumkuchen
More popular here than in its home country, Germany. A prisoner of war made the cake for a food show in Hiroshima in 1919 and his company, Juchheim, is still thriving in Japan.

Strawberry shortcake
Japan's answer to Christmas cake is a fixture in *depachika* (food halls) and cake shops. Strawberries, whipped cream and fluffy sponge. Popular for anniversaries too.

Food halls:
All in one

Much is made of Japan's extraordinary restaurant scene but less well known is the food paradise that is the *depachika*. Derived from the Japanese words for "department store" and "underground", these ubiquitous basement food halls – a feature of almost every department store – are things of wonder.

Sometimes spread across two floors, the *depachika* is an enticing hybrid of daily supermarket, noisy street market and gift shop. Counters are piled high with fresh fish and meat, perfectly ripe melons, *tsukemono* (pickles) and speciality seaweed. Fishmongers shout and vendors offer free samples of chocolates, cheese, ham and *senbei* (rice crackers). Busy workers drop in before closing to grab a quick bento for dinner. Famous restaurants might have a takeaway counter and some even have a few seats.

You'll find delicacies from all over Japan, from Nagasaki *castella* (sponge cakes) to Kyoto green tea, and also goods from further afield: queues form for freshly churned butter from Normandy and pastel-coloured macarons crafted by French patissiers. The best wine shops are often found in *depachika*, where they're stocked with excellent wine and obscure Japanese saké. And since everything is wrapped to perfection, there's nowhere better to get a last-minute gift. Just one piece of advice: don't go on an empty stomach.

Coffee and tea:
Take five

Making and drinking coffee and tea is a chance for workers, families and retirees to have a break, meet and think. We've combed the country for a mix of classic and contemporary spots that have perfected the caffeine fix.

Lawn
Tokyo

Coffee is everywhere in Japan: in cafés, convenience stores and vending machines. For more than a hundred years, the *kissaten* has been at the centre of Japan's coffee business – small cafés up and down the country that offer patrons somewhere to chat, think and read.

Lawn in Tokyo's Yotsuya neighbourhood is a classic, its interior unchanged since 1968. Regulars come to enjoy the simple pleasure of a coffee and a warm omelette sandwich.

Satén
Tokyo

In spite of the coffee boom, *nihon-cha* (Japanese tea) is still ubiquitous. Almost all the tea grown in Japan is green but there are ways of growing and processing it to produce different flavours, including *sencha* (first picking) and *genmaicha* (tea mixed with roasted and popped rice).

Satén, a small tea café in Tokyo, shows that matcha – whisked green tea – can exist beyond the tea ceremony and that *hojicha* (roasted green tea) can work as a latte.

Morihiko
Sapporo

No part of Japan is immune to the coffee craze, even northern Sapporo in Hokkaido, the home of coffee company Morihico. Founded and run by Sapporo-raised graphic designer Sosuke Ichikawa, it started out in 1996 as a standalone coffee shop called Morihiko (spelled with a "k") – an atmospheric space in an old wooden house with a service inspired by the tea ceremony. It has since grown into a large-scale coffee business that includes the Sapporo roastery and café Plantation.

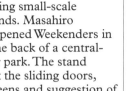

Weekenders Coffee Tominokoji
Kyoto

The new style of coffee in Japan may be a departure from traditional *kissaten* but the care and attention remain the same – even in the country's now thriving small-scale coffee stands. Masahiro Kaneko opened Weekenders in 2016 at the back of a central-Kyoto car park. The stand is tiny but the sliding doors, paper screens and suggestion of a Japanese garden set the scene well. There's no mistaking that you're in the heart of the ancient capital.

Ippodo
Tokyo

Ippodo has been a go-to institution of fine Japanese green tea since it opened its first store in 1717 in Kyoto. The brand's location in Tokyo (*pictured*) is a bright and modern space that sells everything from easy-brew tea bags to the finest *gyokuro* (a shade-grown green tea), matcha starter kits and Japanese-made teapots. Ask the experts at the counter to see what you might fancy; they'll let you try a line-up of teas. If you have time, stop for a while at the site's tearoom.

Clamp Coffee Sarasa
Kyoto

Tucked away in a quiet neighbourhood just to the south of Nijo Castle in Kyoto, Clamp Coffee Sarasa is a rustic oasis in a former gallery space. The exterior is covered with greenery and the dimly lit interior has a DIY feel to it with wooden benches and tables.

The owner has several cafés around the city but the beans are roasted here. On a baking day in Kyoto's hot summer, customers take their coffee iced or order the sharp but refreshing lemon squash.

Little Toy Box
Tokyo

Little Toy Box in the residential neighbourhood of Komaba in Tokyo is a standout among independent cafés. Owner Miki Yamazaki, a former buyer for antique-furniture shops, opened the space in September 2019 after a stint at her favourite café in Tokyo.

Hers is a one-woman operation: she makes coffee and sandwiches and serves every customer herself. She has chosen vintage lamps to complement the white walls of the café, which attracts a loyal clientele.

Drinking:
Liquid lunch

Whatever you're in the mood for – whether it's a highball, a sharp Martini or an award-winning Japanese whisky scrved with a side of jazz – Japan's dimly lit bars have got you covered. Pull up a stool.

Kaku-uchi

Japan has a name for off-licences that let you stay and drink from the bottle that you just bought: *kaku-uchi*. For fans of saké, these bottle-shop-cum-standing-bars are among the best places to try brews from faraway regions.

You go for the drink not the decor – which usually comprises a few tables without chairs set up among the aisles of bottles and refrigerated cases – and many *kaku-uchi* sell small, savoury dishes and snacks. The first *kaku-uchi* are thought to have appeared in the early 20th century near a steel factory in Kitakyushu, in western Japan, and the concept has since spread to every corner of the country.

Once applied to old-fashioned, family-owned off-licences, the term has since expanded to include convenience stores and upscale wine shops that are copying the model to attract an after-work crowd.

○

Bar Martha
Tokyo

The idea of going out for a drink and keeping the conversation to a minimum would put some people off but it's the norm at listening bars in Japan. These establishments attract fans of old-school audio with their collection of vinyl records and analogue hi-fi equipment. Behind the counter, bartenders double as DJs and strictly enforce the house rules: you're here for the music and if you must talk, you're expected to do so quietly.

The country's listening bars gained popularity after the Second World War, when imported records were an extravagance few ordinary consumers could afford. But there has been a resurgence lately. Bar Martha, one of five listening bars that owner Wataru Fukuyama has opened in Tokyo since the 1990s, has records, wooden furniture, dim lighting and the warm sound of two large British-made Tannoy speakers.

○

Brillant
Tokyo

The best Japanese bartenders apply the same level of skill as any craftspeople: ice cubes are skillfully hewn by hand, glasses carefully chosen and cocktails poured with precision. Tokyo's classic hotel bars in particular are staffed by crews who have decades of experience between them. Take Brillant in the Keio Plaza Hotel, for example. Its exposed-brick and swivel-chair interior by designer Riki Watanabe is reason enough to come – and the expertly prepared cocktails will keep you here.

○ Ecru
Fukuoka

At one time, the typical Japanese *tachinomi* (standing bar) was a functional affair – a quick place to grab a drink before heading home for the night. These days the standing bar has been given a makeover.

At Ecru in Fukuoka, the menu could hardly be simpler: coffee, locally baked bread and natural wine, which is big news in Japan these days where palates appreciate the earthy, fermented flavours. Owner Tatsuya Harada opened his popular bar more than a decade ago and, although no more than 20 people can squeeze in, he has a regular clientele and fans who come from far and wide. Harada's presence is key to Ecru's success: he works behind the bar every day, always standing.

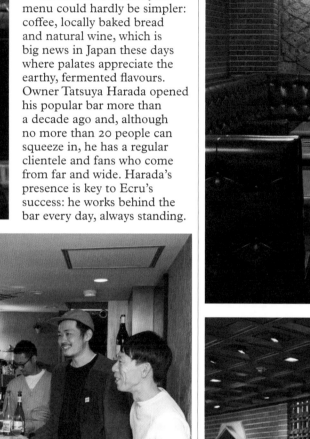

○ Old Imperial Bar
Tokyo

The classic Japanese bar is the antidote to bartending showmanship, intrusive music and flashy design. Instead, these low-lit oases are likely to be staffed by jacketed, bow-tied veterans who know exactly how to execute the perfect Martini – and anything else for that matter.

At the Old Imperial Bar in Tokyo's Imperial Hotel, the interior hasn't changed since 1970; in fact, it features fragments of the hotel's former building, which was designed by Frank Lloyd Wright.

233

Hotels and inns:
Where to hang your hat

Hotels in Japan are run with both passionate precision and a warm spirit of hospitality. Traditional ryokans remain strong while global luxury chains expand, and then there are the innovative capsule hotels.

⊙

Case study: ryokan
Asaba Ryokan

To spend a night in a traditional Japanese inn, known as a ryokan, is to immerse yourself in a unique style of hospitality that has been honed over hundreds of years. There are city ryokan (Kyoto has some of the finest examples) but the ideal inn is found deep within the countryside.

When you arrive you're welcomed by a kimono-wearing *okami* (manager); shoes are left at the door and guests are shown to a room furnished with little more than tatami mats, a low-slung table, two legless chairs and a seasonal painted scroll in the alcove. With any luck there's a hot-spring bath to soak in, preferably outside.

Dinner is a lengthy Japanese feast of fresh local food. The beds are then prepared: cotton futon mattresses are laid out and topped with fluffy quilts and rice-filled pillows.

Asaba Ryokan in Shuzenji, on the Izu Peninsula, has all these qualities: quiet rooms with striking views, an outdoor *onsen* (hot spring) surrounded by bamboo and maple trees, indoor baths made from *koyamaki* (a Japanese pine) and a seasonal menu that might feature grilled sweetfish or *matsutake* (mushrooms). It even has a Noh stage, relocated from a shrine, where traditional performances are held.

Asaba first opened its doors more than 500 years ago and has gradually updated its original format with a spa, a salon serving coffee and champagne, and modern furniture. But for all the tweaks, the essence of traditional *omotenashi* (hospitality) remains strong. For most, one dream-like night is sufficient.

Case study: capsule
Nine Hours

Standing on the eighth floor of the Nine Hours Otemachi capsule hotel is a quintessentially Tokyo experience. Inside the bright-white interior, the mood is clean and quiet. But just beyond the glass wall is an elevated expressway, tall buildings, air-conditioning units and traffic. This thrilling juxtaposition is the last thing you'd expect from a capsule hotel, once seen as no more than a place for salarymen to lay their heads when they missed the last train home.

The capsule hotel had become a tired format before former venture capitalist Keisuke Yui founded the Nine Hours chain and turned a place of last resort into a destination. He opened his first Nine Hours

in Kyoto in 2009, offering guests modern capsules, quality linens, comfortable Japanese mattresses, cotton pyjamas and botanical shower products. He stuck to the basics but made them the best they could be and wrapped them all up in good architecture and sharp graphics. Now he has a string of Nine Hours hotels, including one at Narita Airport.

Yui works with different architects and adapts each hotel to suit its location. This one in Tokyo, designed by Akihisa Hirata, has nearly 130 capsules. Flexibility is key: this hotel is close to the Imperial Palace, whose moat is a popular 5km running circuit, so it rents out kit and welcomes local runners who can drop by and change, shower and nap for less than ¥2,000 (€16). Nine Hours sends out an important message: thoughtful hospitality doesn't have to come with a high price tag.

Case study: global chain
Park Hyatt Tokyo

The Park Hyatt, which arrived in 1994, was one of the first big luxury chains to open in Tokyo. Since then many have followed but it has held its perch at the top; of course, it has the advantage of sitting atop a tower designed by Kenzo Tange, one of Japan's greatest architects.

The hotel appears to be ageless – partly because it's immaculately managed but mainly because it's simply resistant to unnecessary innovation. When it was renovated for its 20th birthday, the updates were so subtle they were barely noticeable; everything was refreshed without being changed.

There are only 177 rooms and, with the explosive boom in visitors to Japan, all are often booked up – not that you would know when you're staying there. A soothing hush encompasses the hotel, whose guest rooms are separated from the hubbub of its bars and restaurants. Many still come to the New York Bar – immortalised in Sofia Coppola's *Lost in Translation* – hoping for a Bill Murray-Scarlett Johansson experience. On a crisp winter morning Mount Fuji provides a spectacular backdrop; at night the hotel switches mood with the lights dimmed as the city outside illuminates.

Retail
商店

Anyone in doubt about the resilience of retail – or the capacity of high streets to anchor neighbourhoods – will find a trip to Japan heartening. Not only has the country remained a manufacturing centre with space on the shelves for time-honoured crafts, it's also making waves.

Over the following pages we'll show you around the top-drawer department stores, dip into our favourite specialist shops and introduce you to the fashion folk who are pressing ahead with desirable innovation. Plus we'll proffer a few fail-safe gift ideas and tasteful souvenirs that will delight even the fussiest of family and friends.

Remember, retail isn't about splashing the cash: it's about creating spaces that show off well-made products and service that keeps customers coming back. Globally we haven't yet reckoned the bill we'll all pay as high streets buckle and physical retail wanes. Japan, however, shows why well-run shops remain an easy sell.

Department stores:
Shopping as spectacle

One of the most mesmerising retail experiences in Japan is visiting a *hyakkaten* (department store). We hit the shop floors of two venerable institutions to find out the secrets of their success.

◉

Isetan Shinjuku
Tokyo

Isetan began life in 1886 as a simple kimono shop. In the 1930s, the enterprise moved to Shinjuku and was transformed into a department store. It may not be the oldest of its kind in Japan – that title belongs to Mitsukoshi (and the two share the same owner) – but no other department store in the country generates as high a profit or pulls in as many shoppers.

Today, Isetan's flagship shop gets millions of visitors a year and makes its mark on Tokyo's retail landscape by turning standard commercial transactions into something special. It's as much about treating everyday walk-ins like VIPs as it is helping customers sift through the shop's vast inventory to find a product that's an exact fit. But the store's basic role remains the same: providing cradle-to-grave products and services and the reassuring quality that the Isetan brand offers.

More than a store
Isetan Shinjuku's top brass try their best to promote the store as an inspiring place that doesn't have to involve going home laden with shopping bags.

Isetan's most cherished customers are the *otokuisama*: big spenders and loyal regulars. There's nothing the staff won't do for them. Looking for custom-made shoes? Isetan will fly in a shoemaker from Italy. Need your shoes shined? The shop will send someone to polish every pair in your wardrobe. The staff aren't salespeople: they're stylists. They can earn fancier titles by taking the initiative to master an ever-changing lineup of brands. There are sommeliers for wines but also towel sommeliers, sleep advisers, shoe counsellors, kimono consultants, professional pillow fitters, baby concierges and a birth-to-death protocol guru who can tell you how much cash to give at a wedding and how long to wait before visiting the graves of deceased family members.

In an industry where the revenues have fallen by a third from a peak of ¥9trn (€73bn) since the early 1990s, novelty sells. Isetan does this with pop-ups and temporary exhibitions that are often set up near the escalators of each floor. When Isetan renovated the main Shinjuku store in 2013 it designated more space for temporary displays. Here you find sample kitchen layouts, books on Japanese folk art, coffee counters and a glass-enclosed classroom where artists run workshops for children. You could spend a lifetime here finding what you need for every occasion and season.

Tokyu Hands
Tokyo

Tokyu Hands is difficult to describe to anyone who's never been there. How do you do justice to a shop that sells everything from pots and pans to planks of wood? Vegetable juicers, earthquake kits and power drills are all here. So too are rucksacks, mattresses, sewing machines and pet supplies. It would be quicker to list what it doesn't sell.

This shop opened in 1978, two years after the company was founded. Tokyu Hands is owned by Tokyu Fudosan Holdings, a property company that was offered the Shibuya land – the site of an old church – and didn't quite know what to do with it. Figuring that in an age of hurtling economic growth and mass production there might be a move back to a more creative, handmade way of doing things, it decided to open a shop that could give people all the tools they needed to fashion their own

life. Hence the store's name and logo: two hands.

Today the Tokyu Hands company, headquartered in Shibuya, has more than 2,700 employees and 57 shops, including five in Singapore, but the Shibuya store is the pulsating heart and historic soul of the business, brimming with creativity and packed to the rafters with products.

The day starts at 10.00 sharp, seven days a week, 364 days a year (only closing for New Year's Day). Staff dressed in green aprons and white

shirts bow as they greet the first customers; you only need to look at their aprons, bursting with tools and notebooks, to know they mean business. In an area so determinedly youthful that J-pop is pumped through the public address system, Tokyu Hands is a beacon of equality. Schoolchildren, local builders, pensioners, art students and tourists pile in, all looking for something different. Pity the hapless visitor who strolls in for a browse. They emerge hours later looking stunned and laden with bags.

It's easy to become obsessed with Tokyu Hands. Spend time here and you realise that this shop documents the preoccupations of Japanese life. The bathing rituals, the love of a massage chair, the need for suitcases with four wheels; in fact, the need for the right piece of equipment to deal with any given situation. Every season, every festival, every event from New Year to the start of the school year puts in an appearance in product form. An anthropologist would have a field day.

Bestsellers
Tokyu Hands' bestselling products would make an interesting history of Japanese fads, from Tamagotchi to cooling gel neckerchiefs. As the rainy season approaches in June, in come the umbrellas; humidifiers are lined up for the winter months. For pollen season there are dozens of masks, drops, nose shields and protective glasses.

245

Specialists:
One-hit wonders

Japan is renowned for its specialist shops, passionate outposts with a singular focus. From high-quality staples and tools for daily life to spaces founded on their owner's eclectic taste, these retailers have mastered the art of doing one thing well.

1.
Ginza Toraya
Tokyo

Fedoras and flat caps, Panamas and baseball caps are just a few of the hats found in the slender interior of Ginza Toraya, which has been in business for more than a century. Among them are classic European brands, including Borsalino, and original releases. According to long-standing shop manager Yujiro Ohtaki, the best hats not only fit well but are an extension of personal style.

2.
Itoya
Tokyo

Itoya's flagship store in Ginza is a celebration of stationery. Spread across two buildings and almost 20 themed floors, the shop has a wide-ranging selection that covers everything from art supplies and postcards to ink pens and handmade paper. Specialist staff including paper concierges, wrapping stylists and pen-repair technicians are on hand to share their knowledge.

3.
Qusamura
Hiroshima

Founded by Hiroshima resident Kohei Oda, Qusamura specialises in plants with personality. He deliberately opted for a spot away from the city centre and the result is a quiet setting in which to browse cacti, succulents and more. Arranged in pots that complement their character, the plants are selected according to their individuality, growth and background.

4.
Towel Shop 441
Tokyo

Yoshii Towel's concept store can be found among Aoyama's designer boutiques. Made in Imabari, a city in southwest Japan long renowned for its towel production, the towels are made using low-pesticide, handpicked Indian cotton. These lightweight, quick-dry towels come in a range of designs and fresh colours; the popular two-tone Chambray line has gauze on one side, pile on the other.

5.
Pigment
Tokyo

Pigment breaks the mould for art supply shops. The Kengo Kuma-designed interior highlights the tools used in the creation process – from pencils to brushes – and one wall is lined with a spectacularly colourful array of bottled pigments for painting. Ongoing research is conducted on-site, while expert-led workshops range from calligraphy and colour philosophy to making your own paints.

6.
Yamabikoya
Fukuoka

Traditional Daruma (wishing dolls) provided the inspiration for Yamabikoya. Artist Shintaro Segawa's shop highlights the various styles and regional nuances of the doll, along with other traditional toys and folk crafts. The space is filled with pieces sourced from makers in the Kyushu region and further afield. Segawa's passion extends to his own hand-painted Daruma, which can be ordered in-store.

7.
Koffee Mameya
Tokyo

The humble coffee bean takes centre stage at Koffee Mameya. Owner Eiichi Kunitomo's selection from Japan and overseas is introduced by baristas who, after a brief consultation, guide customers through the world of light, medium and dark roasts. Serving as a link between roasters and coffee lovers, the shop introduces the finer points of brewing high-quality coffee at home.

8.
Ichihara Heibei Shoten
Kyoto

Established in 1764, Ichihara Heibei Shoten's high-quality chopsticks have gained a loyal following – they are used by everyone from local residents to the Imperial family. The shop is now managed by eighth-generation owner Takashi Ichihara and offers more than 400 varieties of chopsticks – spanning multiple materials, weights and styles – to suit all tastes and needs.

9.
Kama-Asa Shoten
Tokyo

More than a thousand knives line the shelves at Kama-Asa Shoten. Located in Tokyo's kitchenware district, Kappabashi, the retailer sold supplies to the catering industry for more than a century before undergoing a renewal in 2011. The move proved a masterstroke, successfully making its "Made in Japan" kitchenware, high-end tools and professional expertise more accessible to consumers.

10.
Naito Shoten
Kyoto

This long-standing retailer's unmarked shopfront features a range of handcrafted wares, among them brushes, brooms and other cleaning utensils. Made by artisans and workshops throughout Japan, the shop's brushes are designed for specific purposes – including cleaning teapots, tatami mats and kitchenware – and made using materials such as *shuro* (hemp palm) and horsehair.

1
2
3 4
5 6 7 8 9 10

What to buy:
In the bag

It's impossible to visit Japan and return without a slightly heavier suitcase (in fact, we recommend travelling with yours half-empty to begin with). The nation is full of high-quality items that are made to last. Here are our top souvenirs, from fashion and food to craft and crockery.

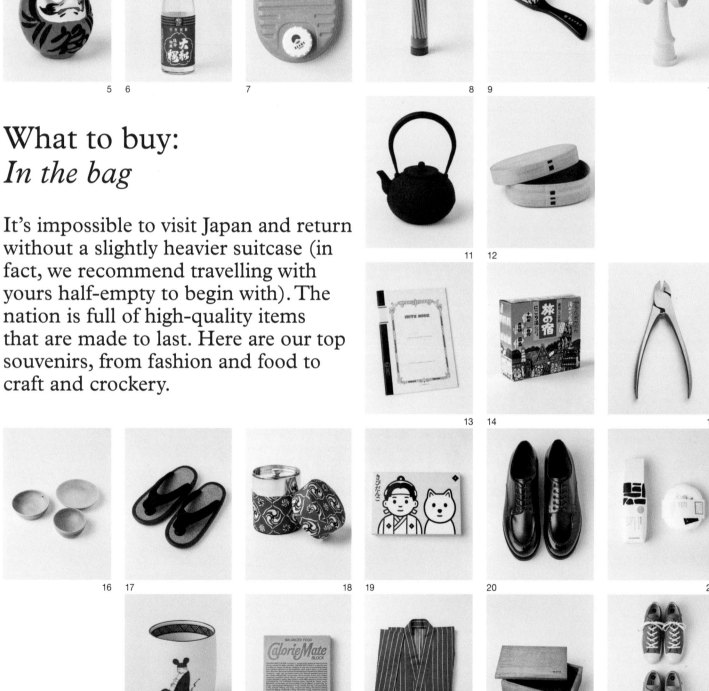

11 12
13 14 15
16 17 18 19 20 21

22 23 24 25 26

1.
Donabe (clay pot) by Shigarakiyaki

2.
Tokkuri flask and *ochoko* (saké cup) by Sodeshigama

3.
Card holder by Kiruna

4.
Pen by Craft Design Technology

5.
Shirakawa Daruma doll

6.
Shochu by Yamatozakura

7.
Hot-water bottle by Maruka × Beams Japan

8.
Incense by Lisn

9.
Hair brush by Edoya

10.
Kendama children's toy from Beams Japan

11.
Nambu tekki (ironware) by Suzuki Morihisa

12.
Magewappa (bentwood) bento by Odate Kougeisha

13.
Notebook by Tsubame Note

14.
Bath salts by Tabinoyado

15.
Nail clippers by Suwada

16.
Wooden bowls by Takahashi Kougei

17.
Sandals by Jojo

18.
Tea caddy from Ginza Takumi

19.
Kibidango rice sweets by Koeido Takeda

20.
Shoes by Yamacho Made

21.
Sweets by Zen Kashoin

22.
Tea cup by Kutani Choemon

23.
Energy bar by Otsuka Pharmaceutical

24.
Yukata by Y & Sons

25.
Butter case by Azumaya

26.
Canvas trainers by Moonstar

27.
Rucksack by Visvim

28.
Bowl by Hakusan Porcelain

29.
Traditional Japanese fan by Marugame Uchiwa

30.
Tenugui (hand towels)

31.
Hair tonic by Yanagiya

32.
Glasses by Eyevan

33.
Tokyo Artrip guidebooks

34.
Oronamin C energy drink

35.
Slippers by Loomer

36.
Kyusu (teapot) by Tosai

37.
Grater by Kobo Aizawa

38.
Japanese towels by Imabari Towel

39.
Leather pinwheel by Hender Scheme

40.
Soap by Kyoshinsha

41.
Vase by Newnormal

42.
Enamel pot by Noda Horo

43.
Scottie Cashmere super-soft tissues

44.
Milk pan by Sori Yanagi

45.
Glasses by Studio Prepa

46.
Foldable umbrella by Montbell

27   28   29

30   31   32   33

34   35   36   37

38   39   40

41   42   43

44   45   46

249

Fashion retailers:
Shop talk

Japan is known for its wealth of high-quality fashion brands but which are leading the pack? Our standouts go above and beyond with their bricks-and-mortar spaces.

ST Company
Gunma

"If you serve truly delicious food in the middle of nowhere, people will come," says Toshio Tamaki, the man behind ST Company, a retailer in the small city of Kiryu which is raising the bar for destination fashion shops. "This rule should apply to fashion too."

The three-storey building is lined with tailor-made racks displaying men's and womenswear from dozens of Japanese and international labels. This all-in-one set-up would be a standout in Tokyo, and the fact that it's in the middle of nowhere is remarkable. Tamaki opened his first shop in Kiryu in 1978 and over the years has travelled the length of Japan to discover new brands. "I have to see everything, clothes and people, face to face," he adds.

United Arrows Roppongi
Tokyo

United Arrows, which was founded in Harajuku in 1989, is now among Japan's biggest fashion retailers. Its flagship store in Tokyo's Roppongi Hills is home to an impressive 550 brands – including UA's own in-house collection – that cater to men and women.

For the interior, UA called on the services of design maestro Masamichi Katayama and his studio Wonderwall, who divided the upper floor into a series of small shops. The gentlemen's formalwear department is wood-panelled, while dark marble lines the walls of the women's salon, which is hung with evening dresses from Rochas and Valentino. UA's luxury Japan-made Junri-an label is displayed in its own traditional Japanese shop, built by master craftsmen and plasterers. Antique watches, leather goods, sunglasses and suitcases are also given their own spaces.

F.I.L. Kyoto/Visvim
Kyoto

Most fashion designers have a vested interest in creating a retail space that best showcases their work – but few are as uncompromising as Hiroki Nakamura, who established his brand Visvim in 2000. Nakamura travels frequently and works with small ateliers around the country on his collections, which include indigo shirts, hand-painted T-shirts and kimono-inspired jackets.

Each shop is testament to Nakamura's perfectionism and Visvim shops – some known as F.I.L. (Free International Laboratory) – are individually designed. Collections are presented against hand-finished white *shikkui* plaster walls. Nakamura, who also has a keen eye for architectural detail, is always drawn to buildings with an interesting past. His F.I.L. store in Kyoto (*pictured*), for example, used to house a 16th-generation doll shop.

Yaeca Home Store
Tokyo

Twelve years and two shops after they started their Tokyo fashion brand Yaeca, Tetsuhiro Hattori and Kyoko Ide wanted to showcase their clothes in a fresh way. They rented a 50-year-old house on a quiet street in the residential district of Shirokane, opened it up and stripped it back to create an unlikely boutique. From the outside, the unmarked house still looks like a home, and customers are greeted with a cup of tea and the smell of baked goods wafting in from the kitchen.

Yaeca clothes are made in Japan and include denim, knits and soft cotton shirts. But fashion occupies only a small part of the spacious house; the rest is taken up by carefully chosen vintage furniture and jewellery, as well as freshly made cakes, fruit juice and honey. Yaeca Home Store welcomes repeat visits as its displays change and different artwork and furniture appear.

251

Ours is one of the oldest and biggest kimono businesses in the country, founded by my great-grandfather in 1917. Originally it was called Yajima Gofukuten (Yajima Kimono Shop) but after the war my grandfather changed it to Yamato, the old name for Japan. When I'm asked if kimonos will survive, I always answer with a confident "yes". But it will take work. We're not simply trying to preserve tradition; we're updating it and keeping it relevant.

We opened a new shop called Y&Sons near Kanda Shrine in 2016. Here we create tailored kimonos that push the boundaries of tradition and can be worn by both Japanese and international customers. We've collaborated on a kimono with Agnès B and made an outdoor model with Snow Peak.

There is more freedom in fashion than there used to be: today, for example, people wear kimonos together with western clothing. After the war, Japanese people felt inferior to their western counterparts but now the country has matured and young people are paying attention. I think by respecting tradition while having some light-hearted fun, we're moving things in the right direction.

Grooming:
Cut above the rest

In the world of men's grooming, the Japanese pursuit of perfection results in barbers with unparalleled skills and hard-to-beat hospitality. Gone are the days when a haircut was just that. We take a seat in three fine establishments.

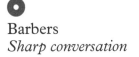

Barbers
Sharp conversation

Japanese barbers strive for excellence and go about their work with proud professionalism. Their attention to detail is close to that of bonsai artists, who prune picture-perfect *matsu* (pine trees) or those who tend Zen gardens.

Octogenarian barber Hiro Matsuda (*pictured*) played a key role in modernising the nation's barber culture. Having honed his skills in London and Paris in the 1970s, including a stint at the Vidal Sassoon hairdressing school, he has won several national and international competitions and received a contemporary master craftsman award from the Japanese government for his peerless technique.

Today, clients head to Matsuda's The Barber – which has outposts across Tokyo – not only for a smart haircut but also to get away from the daily grind. Clients are treated to hot towels and a facial steam while reclining on a deluxe Takara Belmont chair. Heavenly head massages revive the scalp and hot shaves leave skin feeling silky smooth. Dressed in snappy suits, Matsuda's staff can also polish shoes and clean glasses. More often than not, feeling fully refreshed, customers book their next appointment before walking out the door.

Luxury service comes in many different guises. Local barber Cut Salon Ban near Yoyogi Park in Tokyo is packed with everyone from kindergarteners and corporate executives to lively retirees; their shoulder massages and ear cleaning are addictive, and even school children are treated to hot towels. Women come in for *kao sori* (facial shaving) too. Then there's Barber Sakota, a busy neighbourhood spot where you'll find Masaki Sakota, whose two chairs are always full.

Service is always a priority here – no matter the industry. The spirit of hospitality is built into local barbershops as much as it is in the nation's glitziest bars and restaurants.

Service:
Magic touch

Japanese service is like no other and the retail industry is a case in point. From the moment you walk through the door to the moment you leave, customers are treated like royalty and shopping is an experience to remember. You don't have to be a VIP to receive special treatment, and whether you're purchasing a standard pen or a plush suit you'll be greeted with the same amount of respect and care. Here's what you can look forward to.

1.
Take a bow

The politeness and ceremony of bowing can be infectious. From a gentle nod to a deep stoop, this ancient greeting makes you feel honoured and included. You'll find yourself looking forward to entering or exiting an establishment just to partake.

2.
Irasshaimase!

Enter any shop in Japan and you'll hear a startling chorus of "*Irasshaimase!*" (Welcome!). It's a cheery chant that is used everywhere from Uniqlo to department-store food halls, where the competing calls of vendors can sometimes be deafening.

3.
Wheel deal

Shopping with children in tow can be an arduous experience for all involved, which is why good department stores in Japan have complimentary mini prams at the ready. It also keeps the aisles free of toddler reins and sticky mitts.

4.
The gloves are on

The use of white gloves in Japanese retail is widespread, both to protect goods from smudgy fingerprints and also for discreet polishing and buffing. It reveals a level of care for the products you may want to purchase.

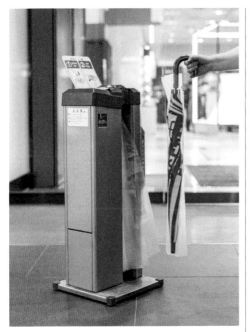

○

5.
Under cover

Japan sees its fair share of rain, particularly during typhoon season. Most shops have a handy device at the entrance that neatly covers your waterlogged umbrella in clear plastic, allowing you to roam around without dripping everywhere.

○

6.
Use protection

Part two of protection against the rain comes at the end of your visit in the form of a clear plastic bag for packaged-up purchases. When skies are grey, your goods will be bundled up before you exit the store.

○

7.
That's a wrap

The less-dextrous among you will be glad to hear that gift-wrapping is a serious business. In fact, a perfectly wrapped box can be as beautiful as its contents. Expect premium paper folded with precision and sealed with a single sticker.

○

8.
Spit spot

Cleanliness is one of the underlying principles of Japanese service – and it's omnipresent in every sector. Everything has to be polished, swept and brushed before the start of the working day. Diligent shopkeepers sweep out front too.

○

9.
Prints charming

Approach the information desk of any shop and you'll discover a suite of printed material, from lookbooks and guide maps to postcards, stickers and bookmarks. Such dedication to print and paper only furthers your in-store experience.

○

10.
Pass the parcel

Don't expect to bag up your own goods when you make a purchase. At the end of the transaction, the shopkeeper will make the effort to personally pass you your shopping bag, often walking around the counter to place it in your hand.

City snapshots
風土

◆

Nearly three-quarters of Japan is sparsely inhabited and the country's population is mostly clustered in cities. Tokyo is top of the pile and remains a magnet for people and wealth (its GDP dwarfs that of many nations). Once you take in the surrounding cities, Greater Tokyo is heading for a spectacular 39 million residents.

If scale were the only measure, you might expect urban life to be a headache. But with an unfathomably low crime rate, swift public transport and an unflappably courteous demeanour, Japanese cities are easy to call home. They also enjoy a diversity of size and climate – ranging from chilly Sapporo in the north to subtropical Naha in the south – while regional identity remains strong. Read on for a flavour of our favourite cities in Japan from the souls who know them best. All aboard.

9

九

Population: 1.97 million
Known for: Sapporo Snow Festival
Speciality dish: *Jingisukan*
(barbecued lamb)

Sapporo.

Sosuke Ichikawa: Ichikawa is the founder and art director of Atelier Morihiko and runs cosy cafés across the city under the Morihico brand.

I was the seventh generation of my family to be born in Tokyo. In the mid-1970s – around the time Japan was at the height of its economic growth – my parents were feeling uncomfortable with the rapid pace of change in the capital and made the decision to relocate to Sapporo on the northern island of Hokkaido. Living in the suburbs of Sapporo during our most impressionable years gave us three boys a sense of freedom that Tokyo simply couldn't offer. My father was a successful graphic designer and it can't have been an easy decision but it was the right one: life here has given me a parallel perspective, an ability to see things from both the centre and the fringes.

The name "Sapporo" is derived from the indigenous Ainu words *sat*, *poro* and *pet* (meaning "dry", "big" and "river"). Sapporo as we know it was only established 150 years ago and there's a pioneering spirit to the city's grid layout and the early Western-style architecture. It is a snowy city (it gets as much as six metres of snow a year) and there is plenty of space: two million people in an area almost twice the size of Tokyo. Drive for two or three hours in any direction and you'll find yourself spoilt for choice in terms of national parks: Daisetsuzan, Shikotsu-Toya and Niseko-Shakotan-Otaru Kaigan are within striking distance. For someone like me who works in the city but spends his free time in the middle of nature, Sapporo is hard to beat.

There is a poem from the Heian period that starts, "Are we not born for play?". I enjoy my work but I also need the nourishment that an outdoor life can offer. For me, Sapporo is the only place in the world where I can have both.

1.
Sapporo is the crab capital of Japan. 'Tarabagani' (red king crabs) are among the most prized
2.
View of Odori Park from Sapporo TV Tower. Odori is the dividing line between the north and south of the city and hosts events such as the famous Sapporo Snow Festival and Sapporo City Jazz, Japan's biggest jazz festival

1

2

1 2

3

4

5

1.
Taking five in Moerenuma Park, which opened in 2005
2.
Sushi restaurant in the lively Nijo Market, where 50 shops sell fresh fish – including crab, 'ikura' (salmon roe) and 'uni' (sea urchin) – as well as agricultural produce
3.
Sapporo TV Tower, built in 1957, offers the best view of the city
4.
Furukawa Hall at Hokkaido University. The latter is known as Hokudai and was founded as Sapporo Agricultural College in 1876
5.
Hokkaido Museum of Modern Art, which opened in 1977
6.
Hokkaido's biggest Shinto shrine was established in 1869, the year the Japanese government gave the old Ainu lands of Ezo a new name, Hokkaido (meaning "road to the north sea")
7.
Sapporo has four distinct seasons, with cool summers, snowy winters and no rainy season
8.
The Former Hokkaido Government Office, built in 1888, was in use for 80 years and is now open to the public
9.
There's plenty of open space for children

6   7

8

9

263

Population: 9.6 million
Known for: Shibuya Crossing, Meiji Shrine and the world's biggest fish market
Speciality dish: *Edomae* (old-Tokyo-style) sushi

Tokyo.

Fiona Wilson: Wilson is MONOCLE's Asia Bureau Chief. She has lived in Tokyo for many years, travelled up and down the country and is still on the hunt for new discoveries.

Tokyo is a city in a permanent state of renewal. Each new tower that goes up – and there are many these days – throws a new perspective on this complex, sprawling metropolis. The rooftop of a skyscraper that recently opened above Shibuya Station offers yet another fresh panorama of the city that takes in the high-rises of Shinjuku, the new National Stadium and the dense green void of Yoyogi Park; far out west, still visible even here, is the perfectly conical presence of Mount Fuji.

Change is part and parcel of life in Tokyo and its citizens are in thrall to novelty. Earthquakes, fires and intense wartime bombing have done their bit to erase the past and yet there is a sense of history in the streets of Tokyo that goes far deeper than the city's modern concrete façade. Many neighbourhoods have the same spidery footprints that appear on maps of the old capital. Born and bred Edokko, as the most deeply rooted Tokyo residents are known, retain the hearty spirit of an older time; in summer, portable shrines are carried around the cramped local streets as they have been for generations.

Tokyo is never any one thing – it's bright lights and soft greenery, epic neon canyons and low-rise residential neighbourhoods, packed commuter trains and quiet coffee shops – and, despite the urban surroundings, a population that clings doggedly (if symbolically) to the seasonal rhythms of the natural world, picnicking under the cherry trees in their thousands in spring. Old and new nudge alongside each other with no sense of dissonance. And perhaps it's the hush that surprises visitors the most. For all its scale, Tokyo somehow retains the civility and charm of a small town.

1.
Overhead expressways are a feature of Tokyo
2.
View from Shinjuku over Yoyogi Park

1

2

1 2

3 4

5

6 7

8 9

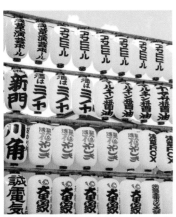

10 11

1.
Soba restaurant in Chofu
2.
Pine trees near the Imperial Palace
3.
Hanasuke flower shop in Meguro
4.
Local festivals are held all over the
city and food stalls are always present
5.
Shinkansen bullet trains travel
all over Japan from Tokyo
6.
Tokyo has tens of thousands of
restaurants and more Michelin stars
than any other city in the world
7.
Even dogs enjoy a ride in a Tokyo taxi
8.
Young couple at a shrine in Asakusa
9.
Plaza in front of Tokyo Station
10.
'Chochin' (paper lanterns) lined up
for a 'matsuri' (festival)
11.
Rainbow Bridge crosses Tokyo Bay
12.
The tuna auction at Tokyo's new fish
market in Toyosu

12

Population: 1.46 million
Known for: Ancient temples and gardens
Speciality dish: *Kaiseki* (traditional multi-course dining)

Kyoto.

Takeshi Ikei: Ikei is the Kyoto-based architect behind Ikei Takeshi Architects. He lives and works in a century-old western-style building that he himself converted.

Go for dinner at someone's house in Kyoto and, come the end of the meal, you may be offered *ochazuke* (a simple rice dish soaked in hot green tea). This, I'm afraid, is your cue to leave. To the uninitiated the tradition might seem unsubtle but in fact it's one of many clever methods used in Kyoto to maintain a happy balance between the public and the private spheres. A diverse mix of people have been gathering here from Japan and beyond for 1,000 years.

Another such practice comes in the form of *Kyo-machiya* (the traditional wooden architecture for which Kyoto is known), in particular the elements that make up the façade: the *koshi* (wooden lattice), *hisashi* (eaves) and *battari shogi* (foldable bench). Today these features are ubiquitous partly on account of their iconic status but their origin was functional: to separate public spaces (roads), which were often overflowing with people, and private spaces (the home). A *koshi*, for example, allows inhabitants to enjoy the view while restricting the peering-in of passers-by, while *hisashi* provide protection from rain and also simply signal the presence of a private property within a public realm.

Like the humble rice dish sometimes served at the closing of a meal, these architectural devices were cleverly designed to navigate the ambiguous boundaries between public and private. Such customs may come across as traditional – even stubbornly conservative – but in fact they are innovative concepts that continue to shape the image of modern Kyoto today. I think it's the beauty of these inventions and the sense of space created by them that give Kyoto its true charm and essence.

1.
Hiyoshiya, the last maker of traditional 'wagasa' (paper umbrellas) in Kyoto
2.
The Zen Buddhist temple of Kinkaku-ji (Golden Pavilion), one of the most famous buildings in Japan

1

2

1.
Bamboo grove in Sagano
2.
'Maiko' – a trainee 'geiko' (geisha) – walking through the Gion neighbourhood
3.
The Kamogawa River runs through the middle of Kyoto
4.
Café at Kaikado, a family-run company that has been making metal tea caddies since 1875
5.
'Oden' (a hearty one-pot dish) at Izakaya Akagakiya
6.
'Karesansui' (dry landscape) at Tofuku-ji temple
7.
'Geta' (wooden sandals) in the courtyard of Fumiyo restaurant in Gion
8.
Traditional 'Kyo-zushi' (Kyoto sushi) restaurant Chidori-tei
9.
Egg sandwich at Smart Coffee, a popular 'kissaten' (coffee shop) that opened in 1932
10.
Picking 'gyokuro' (shaded green tea) in the hilly town of Wazuka, where tea has been grown for more than 800 years; Kyoto is one of the most important tea-growing areas in Japan
11.
Family-owned pottery Asahiyaki in Uji, south of Kyoto, has a 400-year history; this is 16th-generation potter Housai Matsubayashi
12.
Buddhist priest Toryo Ito from Ryosoku-in, a sub-temple of Kennin-ji, Kyoto's oldest Zen temple
13.
Kyoto Imperial Palace; the city was the capital of Japan from 794 to 1868

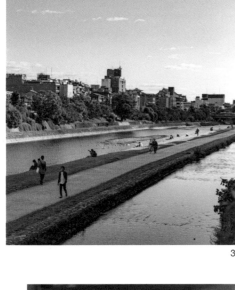

270

9

7 8

10 11

12 13

Population: 2.74 million
Known for: Hanshin Tigers baseball team
Speciality dish: *Kushi-katsu* (deep-fried skewered seafood, meat and vegetables)

Osaka.

Tokuhiko Kise: Osaka native Kise and his wife Hiromi Karatsu founded Truck Furniture in 1997. The business has since expanded, gaining passionate fans nationwide, but they show no sign of leaving their beloved city.

I was born and raised in Osaka and it's here that my business Truck Furniture is based. I've had many offers to expand to Tokyo but I'm happy where I am.

Osaka is a big port city with more than 2.7 million residents, famous neighbourhoods such as Shinsaibashi and Umeda, shopping and nightlife, and hundreds of bridges and canals. But what I love most about this city are the places that a visitor might just overlook.

Those hidden spots are where I mainly eat and drink. Bird, for example, which is my own café and serves doughnuts freshly made with dollops of custard. There's a *kushi-katsu* restaurant called Kushiyoshi that I have been going to for more than 30 years. There's nothing fancy about it but it's exceptionally good. Everything tastes fresh – asparagus, lotus root and shrimp stuffed with shiitake mushrooms – and you eat the *kushi-katsu* with sticky sauce, special salt and mustard, mixed however you like; there are no "rules". I might finish with *mochi* (Japanese rice cakes), which I drizzle with soy sauce and eat while they're still piping hot.

I'm also fond of a tiny bar that's tucked away from the street. Mitsuo, the owner, knows everything there is to know about whisky, and talks about it in a way that's both intriguing and distinctive. It's a special place and just sitting there opens up new worlds by way of conversation. Osaka is full of such pleasures – and that's why I remain.

1.
'Takoyaki' (octopus balls) are an Osaka speciality
2.
A busy street in Dotonbori, one of Osaka's most famous neighbourhoods

1

2

1   2

3

4

5

1.
Retro 'kissaten' Mazura has provided a relaxing refuge for salarymen for 70 years
2.
Yuki Ryu, whose father runs Mazura, is the manager of the old-school bar King of Kings
3.
Outdoor eating
4.
Girls on a school trip
5.
Canal in Dotonbori; neon-lit at night, this is where Hanshin Tigers baseball fans jump into the water after a championship victory
6.
The view from Tsutenkaku Tower, which has been an Osaka landmark for more than 100 years; in the distance is Abeno Harukas, the tallest building in Japan
7.
Ayaka Toyoda at Wad, which sells tea bowls and exhibits contemporary ceramics
8.
Osaka has a reputation for friendliness
9.
Hankyu Umeda is one of the largest department stores in Japan and the Hankyu chain's flagship
10.
Coffee at classic 'kissaten' Mazura

6

7

8

9

10

Population: 1.19 million
Known for: Hiroshima Peace Memorial Park
Speciality dish: *Okonomiyaki* (a savoury pancake)

Hiroshima.

Kengo Nakamoto: Nakamoto is a key figure in the city's culture and fashion scenes, and founder of fashion retailer Ref.

Ours is a city steeped in history. It was here that the Imperial General Headquarters was established to command forces in the First Sino-Japanese War; the Meiji Emperor also briefly relocated to Hiroshima Castle in autumn 1894 and the government temporarily moved with him. Of course, the historic event for which the city is best known was a tragedy. On 6 August 1945 a bomb was dropped on Hiroshima, reducing it to a wasteland.

The building work that followed is a source of great national pride. Japanese architect Kenzo Tange's first major commission was the Hiroshima Peace Memorial Park. And sculptor Isamu Noguchi designed the distinctive handrails for the Peace Bridge, which runs along the park's southern edge. Then there's the Memorial Cathedral of World Peace, designed by Togo Murano which features in Alain Resnais's film, *Hiroshima Mon Amour*.

The rebirth of Hiroshima also brought with it a shift in food culture. Today *okonomiyaki* is a beloved dish in the city, but in 1945 it didn't exist. The burnt fields were contaminated, which meant nothing could be eaten raw. People took the flour distributed by the Allied forces and created a version of *issen yoshoku* (a grilled Kyoto dish), which led to the birth of Hiroshima-style *okonomiyaki*. Now most cafés serve a more polished, modern version but Mori – a charming restaurant on Jizo Dori – remains loyal to the original version.

Like the seven rivers that flow through Hiroshima, fresh ideas continue to course through the city and the youngsters who gather here in the markets, parks and bars are sure to keep Hiroshima innovating, developing and improving long into the future, writing a new history.

1.
Riverside picnic; seven rivers flow through the city down to the Seto Inland Sea
2.
The 16th-century Hiroshima Castle was destroyed by the atomic bomb in 1945 and rebuilt in 1958; it now serves as a museum

1

2

1 2 3

5

4

6 7

8 9

1.
Shunsuke Nomura and Yusuke Yanagida of counter restaurant Lemon Stand Hiroshima
2.
Bar-lined street in Ekinishi, next to JR Hiroshima Station
3.
This branch of Japanese restaurant Rutsubo is 'ichigen-san okotowari' (no drop-ins, invitation-only)
4.
Hiroshima has eight tram lines, the biggest tram network of any Japanese city
5.
'Okonomiyaki' is the most famous local dish – a savoury pancake stuffed with cabbage, noodles, meat and seafood and drizzled with sauce and mayo
6.
Public housing in Motomachi; many survivors moved to this area after the atomic bomb and the government started building the high-rises in 1956
7.
Young fan of the much-loved home baseball team, the Hiroshima Toyo Carp
8.
Hiroshima Castle seen from a high-rise apartment in Motomachi
9.
Genbaku Dome – or the A-bomb dome – is the preserved remains of the former Prefectural Industrial Promotion Hall; it was designated a Unesco World Heritage site in 1996
10.
Hiroshima Electric Railway Co (Hiroden), which runs the city's tram system, was founded in 1910
11.
Bar Ber Bar is a members-only barber shop
12.
Hiroshima Peace Memorial Museum designed by Kenzo Tange in 1955
13.
Hairdressers en route to a cutting contest in the city
14.
The My Way tailoring shop

11

10

12

13 14

Population: 1.59 million
Known for: *Yatai* (outdoor food stands that set up at sunset)
Speciality dish: *Tonkotsu* (pork-bone broth) ramen

Fukuoka.

Koichi Futatsumata: Architect Futatsumata splits his time between Fukuoka and Tokyo, working on interiors, products and houses through his ateliers Case Real and Koichi Futatsumata Studio.

Fukuoka is about quality of life: it has all the shopping, restaurants and nightlife you would expect from a big city and it's close to nature too. There are green spaces such as Ohori Park in the centre and if you drive a little further out you might find yourself walking along a white-sand beach in Itoshima or relaxing in the rural town of Ukiha. These are the city's hidden gems.

Its location is also convenient, especially if – like me – you travel for work. I can leave my office and be at the airport in 30 minutes or catch the Shinkansen and be at a meeting on the other side of the country in a matter of hours; I might even come back the same day. The connection with Asia is strong too. Although modern Fukuoka was founded in 1889, the old city was already the gateway to the rest of Asia – and its cultural influence – as far back as the seventh century.

The residents of Fukuoka work hard but they aren't driven solely by money. They know to set aside time for leisure and the pace is gentler here. Having said that, the city is always quick to pick up on the latest fashion. In fact, there is a particular tolerance for new faces, things and ideas here. I often notice people at *yatai* or izakaya engaging in friendly conversation with those drinking next to them with an ease you don't often find in major cities. Maybe it has something to do with the fact that trade has flourished around the port of Hakata since ancient times. Either way, it's ingrained in the character of the people of Fukuoka to appreciate new things and welcome anyone and anything.

1.
'Takuhatsuso' (mendicant monks) can still be seen in cities across Japan
2.
Sunset view of the city from Fukuoka Tower

1　2

1.
Children playing at
Momochihama beach
2.
Weekend baseball at a primary
school; baseball is Japan's number-
one sport and the city's professional
team is Fukuoka Softbank Hawks
3.
Atsuko Hirano is the proprietor
of popular curry restaurant Floatan
4.
The downtown Tenjin
neighbourhood is the place to
go for shopping and eating
5.
The kimono still has its place in
Japanese life
6.
At night, 'yatai' (outdoor food stands)
line the waterfront in Nakasu; diners
enjoy local food such as 'motsunabe'
(a hot pot made from cow, pig or
chicken intestines)
7.
Gouache Fukuoka sells homeware,
plants and clothes
8.
Pockets of greenery and mini
playgrounds are a feature of densely
populated Japanese cities
9.
Rikiya Yokoo, buyer at Spares, which
sells vintage clothes and cars
10.
The classic Toyota Crown taxi
11.
Ichiran Ramen started in Fukuoka
in 1960 and specialises in pork-bone
broth 'tonkotsu'
12.
Tlalli sells casual clothes and coffee
13.
Dazaifu Tenmangu, the largest shrine
in Fukuoka, is dedicated to learning,
culture and the arts
14.
Convenience stores are omnipresent
in Japan – even in stations

3　　　　　　　　　　　　　　　　4

5　　　　　　　　　　　　　　　　6

8

7

9

10   11

12

13   14

Population: 595,000
Known for: Sakurajima volcano
Speciality dish: *Kurobuta*
(black pig) pork

Kagoshima.

Hitoshi Okamoto: Tokyo-based
editor Okamoto hails from Hokkaido
but has written insightful guides
to Kagoshima.

The first time I visited Kagoshima I was
invited to a friend's home, and as we sat
around eating local confectionery in the
garden, Sakurajima erupted. A plume of
smoke rose to a considerable height from
the summit, which was clearly visible in
the distance. It was shocking for me to
learn that Sakurajima is still such an active
volcano but even more so that no one aside
from me – a non-native of the prefecture
– seemed to care. Sakurajima has erupted
at least once every year since 1955, and in
some years nearly 1,000 times, which is
why – I suppose – a minor belch like this
didn't even cause my companions to look
up from their sweets.

Sakurajima shapes the fundamental
personality of the people who live in
Kagoshima. They appear to be very
laid-back but when something happens
they are quick to act, co-operating and
concentrating their enormous energy to
resolve the issue. They are my role models
for reclaiming a more human pace of
life, something I had lost with my fast-
moving Tokyo lifestyle.

I believe the people of this city are
the descendants of those who travelled
great distances on the Kuroshio current
from the south in the distant past. There
is a sense that Kagoshima is an extension
of the island chain which runs all the
way from Indonesia through Taiwan
and Okinawa (formerly Ryukyu) to
this southernmost tip of the Japanese
mainland. Though each of these island
nations has its own unique culture, the
same blood seems to pump through all
their veins and Kagoshima somehow feels
connected to that, giving it an identity
unlike that of any other city in Japan.

1.
Photo opportunity at Sengan-en,
a 17th-century villa and garden
that once belonged to the
Shimazu family
2.
View of Kagoshima and Sakurajima,
one of Japan's most active volcanoes

1 2

3

4

5

6 7

8

1.
The Kotsukigawa River with Sakurajima beyond
2.
Dining out in Kagoshima
3.
Tram passing in front of Yamagataya, Kagoshima's original department store; the city has had trams since 1912
4.
'Janbo mochi', a traditional Kagoshima sweet made from pounded rice and served with two bamboo skewers, at Hirataya
5.
Susumuya green-tea shop was founded in 2012 by Kotaro Shinbara, whose family has been in the tea business for generations
6.
Shrine maiden at Terukuni Shrine, founded in the 19th century and the most important Shinto shrine in the city
7.
A truck at Kagoshima's busy fish market; fish comes from Kinko Bay and beyond and includes sea bream, flying fish and 'kamenote' (literally "turtle's hand"; in fact a Japanese barnacle with crab-like flesh)
8.
Kazuhiro Arakawa, barman at Ikeda, the oldest bar in Kagoshima
9.
The Sakurajima Ferry plies the short route between the city and Sakurajima 24 hours a day
10.
Kagoshima is the home of shochu, which is distilled from rice, sweet potatoes, barley or brown sugar; Higashikawa sells a wide selection
11.
Kenta and Maki Hayashi from Hay Grill & Coffee
12.
Kagoshima is often compared to Naples; Sakurajima is an active volcano and regularly puffs out smoke and ash
13.
Tram stop in front of Kagoshima Station

9   10

11   12   13

Population: 321,920
Known for: Subtropical climate
Speciality dish: *Goya Champuru*
(bitter-gourd stir-fry)

Naha.

Ryoma Yabu: Former architecture student Yabu runs Ploughmans Lunch Bakery, a popular café in an old US military house in Okinawa.

In October 2019 the main hall of Naha's Shuri Castle – a Unesco World Heritage site dating back to the ancient Ryukyu Kingdom – was razed to the ground by a fire. It's not the first time it has suffered widespread destruction: it was bombed during the Second World War and through restoration works became an enduring symbol of both Okinawa and its people's struggle to overcome adversity. Its loss gave the residents of this island community fresh cause to look back to their roots.

I was born and raised in Tokyo and moved to Okinawa at the age of 22 but my father was from Naha so we spent many childhood holidays there. I developed a fond admiration for the bright, individualistic people of the prefecture with their sunny disposition, no doubt fostered by the warm climate and tropical landscape – sandy beaches lapped by emerald waters tend to have that effect.

The natural environment has also had a strong influence on Naha's architecture. The hot, humid climate and threat of typhoons mean that constructing in concrete is the norm, and the once-vivid-now-faded, box-shaped homes are reminiscent of the work of both Luis Barragán and Tadao Ando.

In recent years many people have relocated to Okinawa from the mainland and some of the region's distinctive flavour is arguably starting to fade. But the blend of influences is also creating an entirely new culture. Take coffee for example: Okinawa is one of the few coffee-bean production areas in Japan and Naha is now home to several world-class roasters and exceptional coffee stands. So, it may be respectful of its roots but this city is no stranger to renewal.

1.
American-import clothes shop Linaka
2.
'Shisa' are a common sight on rooftops in Naha; somewhere between a lion and a dog, these mythical guardians are a feature of Ryukyu (Okinawan) culture

1

2

289

1 2

3

4

5 6

290

7

8

9 10

1.
Walls of Shuri Castle
2.
Thousands of US marines and military personnel are stationed in Okinawa
3.
Timeless Chocolate in Chatan sells chocolate made with cacao beans and Okinawan sugar cane
4.
Cocoroar Café is housed in a former military home, one of many retro concrete bungalows that have become highly sought-after
5.
The Okinawan Urban monorail, known as Yui Rail, runs for 17 kilometres from Naha Airport
6.
Okinawans' longevity has been attributed in part to the traditionally vegetable-rich diet
7.
Tropical Beach in Ginowan, a 30-minute drive from Naha
8.
Shunji Fujita, owner of the Okinawan craft shop Garb Domingo
9.
Komesen, one of a number of izakaya that open at night in Makishi market
10.
For all kinds of Okinawan foods – from sea grapes and 'goya' (bitter gourds) to 'rafute' (pork belly) and fresh fish – people head to Makishi
11.
Makiminato branch of the American fast-food chain A&W
12.
Orion is the classic Okinawa beer (founded in 1957) but microbreweries such as Ukishima Brewing, which is making beer in the heart of Naha, are popping up

11

12

モノクル日本全集

The Monocle Book of
JAPAN

Acknowledgements

**The Monocle
Book of Japan**
EDITOR
Fiona Wilson

ASSOCIATE EDITORS
*Kenji Hall
Joe Pickard
Junichi Toyofuku*

DESIGNERS
*Richard Spencer Powell
Giulia Tugnoli*

PHOTO EDITOR
Shin Miura

PRODUCTION
*Jacqueline Deacon
Sarah Kramer*

PRINCIPAL PHOTOGRAPHERS
*Kohei Take
Taro Terasawa*

Special thanks:
*Robert Bound
Josh Fehnert
Rie Kabata
Brenda Kaneta
Amy Richardson
Yoshitsugu Takagi*

Researchers:
*Gabriele Dellisanti
Audrone Fiodorenko
Josh Greenblatt
Hester Underhill
Julia Webster
Zayana Zulkiflee*

CHAPTER EDITING:
An illustrated grand tour
*Shin Miura
Joe Pickard*

Portrait of a Nation
*Shin Miura
Joe Pickard
Fiona Wilson*

Culture
Kenji Hall

Design and architecture
*Junichi Toyofuku
Fiona Wilson*

Transport
Kenji Hall

Business
Kenji Hall

Meet the people
Hester Underhill

Hospitality
*Junichi Toyofuku
Fiona Wilson*

Retail
*Junichi Toyofuku
Fiona Wilson*

City snapshots
*Shin Miura
Joe Pickard
Fiona Wilson*

Monocle
EDITORIAL DIRECTOR
& CHAIRMAN
Tyler Brûlé

EDITOR IN CHIEF
Andrew Tuck

CREATIVE DIRECTOR
Richard Spencer Powell

EDITOR
Molly Price

DEPUTY EDITOR
Amy van den Berg

DESIGNERS
*Sam Brogan
Jessica-North Lewis
Oli Kellar*

PHOTO EDITORS
*Matthew Beaman
Alex Milnes
Amara Eno
Kamila Lozinska*

PRODUCTION
*Jacqueline Deacon
Sarah Kramer*

Photographers:
Masanori Akao
Alexis Armanet
Masashi Asada
François Cavelier
Alex Cretey Systermans
Keisuke Fukamizu
Brian Guido
Shimpei Hanawa
Motohiko Hasui
Satoko Imazu
Sayuki Inoue
Shinichi Ito
Kentaro Ito
Tetsuya Ito
Hiroshi Kai
Ryo Kaikura
Tetsuo Kashiwada
Kyoko Kataoka
Yoshio Kato
Masakazu Kuroiwa
Tamotsu Kurumata
Takafumi Matsumura
Hayato Noge
Tetsuya Ochi
Kohichi Ogasahara
Jun Okada
Ben Richards
Christoffer Rudquist
Masahiro Shoda
Arata Suzuki
Kohei Take
Taro Terasawa
Miwa Togashi
Jonathan Vdk
Tsutomu Watanabe
Norito Yamauchi
Fuminari Yoshitsugu

Writers:
Robert Bound
Tyler Brûlé
Ben Davis
Koichi Futatsumata
Kenji Hall
Sosuke Ichikawa
Takeshi Ikei
Tokuhiko Kise
Kengo Nakamoto
Hitoshi Okamoto
Mark Schilling
Richard Spencer Powell
Junichi Toyofuku
Andrew Tuck
Hester Underhill
Fiona Wilson
Ryoma Yabu
Takayuki Yajima

Images:
Asahi Shimbun
Getty Images
Nobutada Omote
Shigeo Ogawa
Teshima Art Museum/Rei Naito:
Matrix, 2010/Ken'ichi Suzuki
Alamy
Pixta
Shutterstock

Illustrator:
Satoshi Hashimoto

Stylist:
Shun Katakai

Index

A

ACROS Fukuoka,
 Fukuoka 110—111
Adachi Museum of
 Art, *Yasugi*
 44—47
Air Track, *Osaka*
 90—91
All Nippon Airways
 uniforms 191
Ando, Tadao
 58—59, 165
Appliances 173
Art pavilion
 at Shinshoji
 Zen Museum
 and Gardens,
 Fukuyama 145
Asaba Ryokan,
 Shuzenji 234—235
Asahikawa
 174—175
Auralee 250

B

Bake (company)
 194
Bar Martha,
 Tokyo 232
Barber Sakota,
 Tokyo 254
Barber, The,
 Tokyo 254
Barbers 254—255
Bars 232—233
Baseball 60—63

Baumkuchen 227
Bikes 184
Boats 185
Bonsai 50—51
Bonenkai
 Season 156
Books 152—153
Brillant, *Tokyo* 232
Buddhism 52,
 58—59
Bunkitsu, *Tokyo* 152
Burger and pizza
 joints 221
Business success
 stories 194—201
Butterfly stool 176

C

Camelback,
 Tokyo 36
Cafés 36—37,
 230—231
Cars 186—187
Chasen 177
Chochin 176
Church of the
 Light, *Ibaraki* 165
Cinema Amigo,
 Zushi 146
Cinemas 146
Clamp Coffee
 Sarasa, *Kyoto* 231
Cleaning staff 183
Comoli 250
Coastguard recruits,
 Kure 208—209

Construction
 workers 102
Counter dining 221
Craft 178—179
Cut Salon Ban,
 Tokyo 254

D

Daikanyama
 Tsutaya Books,
 Tokyo 152
Date, Miwako
 214—215
Densuke Shoten,
 Naha 96—97
Depachika
 228—229
Design icons
 176—177
Dogs 136—138,
 206—207

E

Ecru, *Fukuoka* 233
Ekiben 225
Ella Records,
 Tokyo 155
Enamelware 178
Engineered Bike
 Service, *Kyoto* 184
Especial Records,
 Osaka 155

F

F.I.L. Kyoto/
 Visvim, *Kyoto* 251
Fabric 179
Family restaurants
 224—225
Fashion retailers
 250—251
Festivals 155
Film 146—147
Fire brigade
 volunteer 212
First Sino-Japanese
 War 276
Food halls 228—229
Fruit parfait 227
FT Architects 162
Fuglen, *Tokyo* 37
Fukuda, Kiju 28
Fukuoka 12,
 110—111, 221,
 233, 247,
 280—283
Fukuyama 145
Futatsumata,
 Koichi 280

G

Gardeners 103
Ginza Toraya,
 Tokyo 246
Gold leaf 179
Gunma 250
Gyoza 227

H

Hakone 22—23, 25
Hakone Retreat
 Före, *Hakone*
 22—23, 25
Hamburg steak with
 Napolitan 227
Hanayashiki, *Tokyo*
 92—93
Haneda Airport,
 Tokyo 86—87,
 190
Hanshin Tigers
 60—63
Hender
 Scheme 250
Hiking 38—40
Hill of the Buddha,
 Sapporo 58—59
Hiroshima 13, 246,
 276—279
Hokkaido 16—17,
 174—175, 260
Honda Super
 Cub 176
Hotel New Grand,
 Yokohama 27
Hotels and inns
 234—239
Hyakkaten
 242—245

I

Ibaraki 165
Ichihara Heibei
 Shoten, *Kyoto* 247
Ichikawa, Sosuke
 260
Ichinomiya Danchi,
 Takamatsu 76
Ikei, Takeshi 268
Inflight food 190
Ippodo 231
Ise 168—169
Ise Shrine, *Ise*
 168—169
Isetan Shinjuku,
 Tokyo 242—243
Ishinomaki
 Laboratory 201
Itoya, *Tokyo* 246
Izakaya 220

J

J-pop 154
JPN Taxi 187

K

Kabuki 153,
 216—217
Kagawa Prefectural
 Budokan,
 Takamatsu
 68—69

Kagawa Prefectural Office East Building, *Takamatsu* 168
Kageoka no Ie, *Tokyo* 116—117
Kagoshima 12, 284—287
Kaku-uchi 232
Kama-Asa Shoten 247
Kanazawa 14
Karaoke 156—157
Karate 204—205
Karesansui 44—49, 176
Katsu Sando 226
Katsura Rikyu, *Kyoto* 163
Keirin 184
Kigurumi.biz, *Miyazaki* 135
Kikutake, Kiyonori 167
Kimono 28, 179, 252—253
Kise, Tokuhiko 272
Kissaten 32—35, 230
Koban 100—101
Kobe 144
Koen Dori, *Tokyo* 88—89
Koffee Mameya, *Tokyo* 247
Kogakuin University Archery Hall, *Tokyo* 162

Koreeda, Hirokazu 147
Korokke 226
Koshien, *Nishinomiya* 60—63
Kumamon 196—197
Kumiko screens 179
Kure 208—209
Kurokawa, Kisho 166
Kyoto 14, 146, 163, 164—165, 184, 231, 236—237, 247, 251, 268—271
Kyoto International Conference Centre, *Kyoto* 164—165
Kyushu 12, 112—115

L

Lacquer 178
Ladrio, *Tokyo* 33
Lawn, *Tokyo* 32, 230
Lawson 199
Line (company), *Tokyo* 149
Little Toy Box, *Tokyo* 231
Living National Treasures 28—29

M

Machiya 73
Magazine House, *Tokyo* 149
Magazines 150—151
Makunouchi bento 226
Mama-chari 184
Mameshin, *Otsu* 20—21
Manga 153
Maru (Shiba) 206—207
Matsuri 54—55
Matsuyama 13
Media 148—149
Meiji, *Tokyo* 126—127
Meishi 198
Melon pan 227
Metalwork 179
Miidera, *Otsu* 22—23
Milet 216
Mitsubishi Electric, *Tokyo* 124—125
Mitsubishi SpaceJet M90 190
Miyazaki, Hayao 147
Moonstar 201
Mori Building Digital Art Museum: TeamLab Borderless, *Tokyo* 142—143

Morihico 230, 260
Morihiko, *Sapporo* 230
Muji 177, 195
Muji House 195
Muji hut 177
Musashino 152
Musashino Place library, *Musashino* 152
Museums 142—145
Music 154—155
Muu-chan 134

N

Nabe 227
Nagasaki 12
Naha 12, 96—97, 288—291
Naito Shoten, *Kyoto* 247
Nakamoto, Kengo 276
Nakamura, Yoshiaki 87
National newspapers 148
National Art Centre Tokyo, The, *Tokyo* 166
Nasu 170—171
Nezu Museum, *Tokyo* 145
Nikkei, The 148—149
Nine Hours, *Tokyo and Kyoto* 236—237

Nishinomiya 60—63
Nishizawa, Ryue 161
Noguchi, *Isamu* 176, 276

O

Obama Kodomoen, *Kyushu* 112—115
Oden 226
Okamoto, Hitoshi 284
Okinawa 12, 96—97, 288—291
Okura Tokyo, *Tokyo* 26, 78—79
Old Imperial Bar, *Tokyo* 233
Olympus Pen EE-2 176
Omiya Bonsai Village, *Saitama* 50—51
Omuraisu 34, 226
1964 Olympics poster 176
On the street 188—189
Onigiri 227
Onsen 24, 25
Osaka 13, 90—91, 155, 272—275
Otani Sachio 164—165
Otsu 20—23

P

Paper (craft) 178
Park Hyatt, *Tokyo* 238—239
Parks 106—111
Pedestrian bridges 104—105
Pigment, *Tokyo* 247
Pignon, *Tokyo* 303
Planes 190—191
Porcelain 179
Pottery 178
Pruning scissors 177

Q

Qusamura, *Hiroshima* 246

R

Rajio taiso 124—127
Ramen 227
Randoseru 177
Residences 170—175
Ryokan 234—235

297

Index

S

Sacai 250
Saitama 50—51
Saké 56—57, 94—95
Sakurajima, *Kagoshima* 284, 285, 286, 287
Salary men 118—121
Sanma-no-shioyaki 226
Sano boats 185
Sapporo 17, 58—59, 106—107, 230, 260—263
Satén, *Tokyo* 230
Schilling, Mark 147
Sea Paseo 185
Sejima, Kazuyo 160
Sendai 16
Sensu 176
Service 256—257
Setouchi Seaplanes 191
Shibuya Publishing & Booksellers, *Tokyo* 303
Shigemori, Mirei 48—49
Shikoku 13
Shinjuku Gyoen, *Tokyo* 108
Shinkansen 80—81, 182—183
Shinto 41, 52—57, 64, 169

Shirakawa-go 42—43
Shobodanin 212
Shrines 41, 52—57, 169
Shuri Castle, *Naha* 288, 291
Shuzenji 234—235
Soy-sauce dispenser 177
Specialist shops 246—247
ST Company, *Gunma* 250
Stationmaster 214
Stations 183
Strawberry shortcake 227
Sumida Hokusai Museum, *Tokyo* 160
Sumo 64—67
Sushi 226
Suzuki Jimny 187

T

Tabloids 149
Tada, Jun 212—213
Takamatsu 76, 168
Takano, Mahiro 204—205
Takenaka Carpentry Museum, *Kobe* 144
Takoyaki 226
Tamago-sando 34, 36

Tange, Kenzo 76, 168, 230, 276
Tatami mat 177
Tateyama–Kurobe Alpine Route 38—40
Taxis 82—84, 187
Tea ceremony 30—31
Tei zaisu 177
Temples 22—23
Tempura 224, 226
Tempura restaurants 224
Teshima 161
Teshima Art Museum, *Teshima* 161
Theatre 153, 216—217
Tokyo 15, 26, 32, 33, 36, 37, 78—79, 86—89, 92—95, 108, 116—117, 124—125, 126—127, 138, 142—143, 145, 146, 149, 152, 155, 160, 162, 166, 172—173, 185, 190, 210—211, 230, 231, 232, 233, 236—237, 238—239, 242—243, 244—245, 246, 247, 250, 251, 254, 264—267, 303

Tokyo Metropolitan Park Association, *Tokyo* 210—211
Tokyo Shouten, *Tokyo* 94—95
Tokyo Water Taxi 185
Tokyu Hands, *Tokyo* 244—245
Toto toilet 177
Toukouen Hotel, *Yonago* 167
Towel Shop 441, *Tokyo* 246
Toyota Century 186
Trains 80—81, 182—183
Truck Furniture, *Osaka* 272

U

Udon shops 222—223
Udon taxi driver 212—213
Uniqlo 198
United Arrows Roppongi, *Tokyo* 250
Uplink, *Tokyo and Kyoto* 146

V

Vending machines 94—95
Vinyl shops 155

W

Wagyu steak 226
Waltz, *Tokyo* 155
Weekenders Coffee Tominokoji, *Kyoto* 231
What to buy 248—249
What to order 226—227
Woodwork 178

Y

Yabu, Ryoma 288
Yaeca Home Store, *Tokyo* 251
Yajima, Takayuki 252
Yakitori 227
Yamabikoya, *Fukuoka* 247
Yamagata Design 194
Yamase, Shoin 28—29
Yamato (kimonos) 252
Yamato postal service 200

Yamatomichi 199
Yasugi 44—45
Yatai 96—97
Yokohama 27
Yonago 167
Yoshida, Morihide 206
Yoshoku 227
Yoyogi Park, *Tokyo* 138, 303
Yuru-kyara 132—135, 196—197

Z

Zaru soba 227
Zushi 146

About Monocle:
Magazine and more

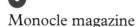

Monocle magazine

MONOCLE magazine is published 10 times a year, including two double issues (July/August and December/ January). We also produce annual specials such as our global lookahead, *The Forecast*, and business title, *The Entrepreneurs*. Look out for our seasonal weekly newspapers too.

Monocle Radio

Our round-the-clock internet radio station delivers global news and shows covering foreign affairs, urbanism, business, culture, food and drink, design and print media. You can listen live or download from *monocle.com/ radio* – or wherever you get your podcasts.

Books

Since 2013, MONOCLE has been publishing books such as this one, covering a range of topics from home design and travel to how to live a gentler life, to our country-focused guides. All our books are available on our website, through our distributor Thames & Hudson or at all good bookshops.

Monocle Minute

MONOCLE's smartly appointed family of newsletters come from our team of editors and bureaux chiefs around the world. From the daily Monocle Minute to the Monocle Weekend Edition and our weekly On Design special, sign up to get the latest in lifestyle, affairs and design, straight to your inbox every day.

In 2007, MONOCLE was launched as a monthly magazine briefing on global affairs, business, design and more. Today we have a thriving print business, a radio station, shops, cafés, books, films and events. At our core is the simple belief that there will always be a place for a brand that is committed to telling fresh stories, delivering good journalism and being on the ground around the world.

We're Zürich and London-based and have bureaux in Tokyo, Bangkok and Los Angeles, with others on the horizon. Over the years our editors and correspondents have come to understand what makes a nation tick. This knowledge is unpacked in this book and throughout our reporting on Monocle Radio, in film at *monocle.com* and, of course, across our print products.

Tokyo Bureau:
Monocle in Japan

1

When MONOCLE launched in 2007, Tokyo was the magazine's sole bureau in Asia. Over the years the team has travelled the length and breadth of the country, interviewing politicians, actors, potters, architects, fashion designers, saké brewers, sumo stars and a long list of others. There was the collector of old wooden buildings in Kyushu; the cold-weather combat-training unit of the Self-Defence Force in the mountains of Hokkaido; the green-fingered gardener who is responsible for looking after Tokyo's many cherry trees. And then there have been any number of non-human subjects, from dogs to furry mascots. It's been a blast.

Where to find us
You'll find the Tokyo bureau in Tomigaya, a friendly neighbourhood tucked away between Shibuya and Yoyogi Park and close to NHK, Japan's national broadcaster. This low-key area has many attractions: restaurants, bakeries and a cluster of good coffee shops among them. It's easy to find the shop and the bureau is there too, hidden behind the sliding doors.

Our hard-working team reveal three local spots that they have got to know and love.

Pignon

Many glasses of wine have been shared in this cosy bistro conveniently located on the same road as the bureau. Owner Rimpei Yoshikawa is a stellar chef, cooking up juicy roast pork and delicious salads.

Shibuya Publishing & Booksellers

Fifteen minutes spent browsing in this small bookshop is enough to provide inspiration on subjects ranging from architecture to travel and cooking. NAP Architects did a good job with the interior too.

Yoyogi Park

Tokyo isn't overloaded with green spaces but this is one of the biggest. Rain or shine it has much to offer: you can jog, hire a bike, admire the pedigrees in the dog run or just take a head-clearing stroll.

1.
Browse magazines and collaborations in the Monocle Shop
2.
Work in progress: *The Monocle Book of Japan*
3.
In discussion at the bureau
4.
The Monocle Shop is in the charming Tomigaya district
5.
Reporting for Monocle Radio

2   3

THE MONOCLE SHOP

4

5

303

Thank you
Arigato